MICHAEL SCHUMACHER

Formula for Success

MICHAEL SCHUMACHER

FORMULA FOR SUCCESS

THE GRIPPING INSIDE STORY
OF ONE OF MOTOR RACING'S
GREATEST CHAMPIONS

DERICK ALLSOP

Ebury Press
LONDON

AUTHOR'S ACKNOWLEDGEMENTS

This book has been compiled with the assistance and forbearance of a great number of people and to all those, whether or not they are mentioned here, I wish to convey my sincere thanks. Above all I would like to place on record my appreciation for the frank interviews and generous co-operation given to me by Michael Schumacher, and for the help and encouragement of his press officer, Heiner Büchinger. My thanks also go, in no particular order, to Rolf Schumacher, Eddie Jordan, Martin Brundle, Willi Weber, Jochen Mass, Alain Prost, Derek Warwick, Riccardo Patrese, Damon Hill, Ross Brawn, Niki Lauda, Heinz-Harald Frentzen, John Barnard, Luca di Montezemolo, Gerhard Berger, Jane Nottage, Jean Todt, Di Spires, Giancarlo Baccini, Ray Matts and Stan Piecha. Finally, I am hugely indebted to the team at Ebury Press, Gillian Haslam, Behram Kapadia and in particular, Margaret Little, whose enthusiasm and tenacity have been crucial to this project.

First published in 1996 by Ebury Press

1 3 5 7 9 10 8 6 4 2

Copyright © Derick Allsop

Derick Allsop has asserted his right to be identified as Author of this Work.

Ebury Press
Random House, 20 Vauxhall Bridge Road,
London SW1V 2SA

Random House Australia (Pty) Limited
20 Alfred Street, Milsons Point, Sydney,
New South Wales 2061, Australia

Random House New Zealand Limited
18 Poland Road, Glenfield,
Auckland 10, New Zealand

Random House South Africa (Pty) Limited
PO Box 337, Bergvlei, South Africa

Random House UK Limited Reg. No. 954009

A CIP catalogue record for this book is available from the British Library

ISBN 0 09 182791 4

Picture Editor and Designer: Behram Kapadia

Printed and bound in Spain by Printer Industria Grafica, Barcelona

Contents

A Message from Michael

I am fortunate that racing, my great love since I was a small boy, has become my profession and a rewarding one at that. But above all I am gratified that the fun I first discovered at my local kart track, all those years ago, remains for me the single, most inspiring appeal of the sport. I hope this becomes evident in the pages that follow because, much as I have endeavoured to fulfil myself in terms of achievement on the track and my career has inevitably brought me into contact with controversy, my love and faith in the simple pleasures of driving a kart or a car are undiminished.

I would like to take this opportunity to thank all those who have helped and supported me in my career. Their backing and encouragement has been a constant source of strength. I hope this book will give all fans an insight into the life of a racing driver and the world of Formula One. If you find the words a little heavy going, you can still look at the pictures!

Best wishes

Michael Schumacher

Introduction

Another bleak, winter's morning, another test session in the unending work schedule of a Grand Prix motor racing team. The pursuit of excellence and glory is generated at scenes such as this, in front of empty grandstands and unseen by the millions who follow the World Championship races through the summer on television.

This time the stage is the Paul Ricard Circuit, perched in the bleached hills of Provence, and this time the team setting up camp is Ferrari. It is supposed to be a strictly private operation, off-limits to the media, but little moves under the banner of the sport's most famous marque unattended by press and film crews. Nothing about Ferrari is modest or unobtrusive. They have hired the track, with all its requisite safety organisation and personnel, for their sole use at the three-day test. They have three trucks to transport the equipment and a motorhome.

Opposite The man carrying Ferrari's hopes.
Below Bleak day, empty stands... the loneliness of winter testing.

8

They have also lavished a fortune for the services of a man who has attracted even greater than usual interest to the stable of the Prancing Horse. Michael Schumacher, world champion for the previous two seasons, is Ferrari's new No. 1 driver; the man they hope will galvanise the team in the way he did at Benetton and deliver the crown to Italy for the first time since Jody Scheckter's success in 1979.

Now, at the dawn of 1996, Schumacher is about to make his first appearance in the red race-suit of Ferrari and the pictures from here will represent another landmark in the remarkable career of this sportsman. Between stints in the car and technical briefings, he poses for the photographers beneath mercifully clearing skies and answers a barrage of questions to camera.

Jochen Mass, former team-mate.

Surveying all with a patron's countenance is Jochen Mass, a former Grand Prix driver, once Schumacher's colleague in the Mercedes sportscar team and, like his fellow German, based a couple of hours' drive along the Côte d'Azur, in Monaco.

'Coming to Ferrari is a good move for Michael,' Mass says, unequivocally. 'He has done all there is to do at Benetton. There was nothing left for him there. He needs this new challenge in his career, and Ferrari needs him. It is also a good move for them. You can see the difference already. He will bring them all together, make them focused, and of course he will give them everything. But perhaps most importantly of all, this move is good for Formula One. It makes Ferrari a true challenger again, to compete with Williams and Benetton. We could have a fantastic Championship.'

In little more than four years as a Grand Prix driver, Schumacher confirmed his potential as the natural successor to Alain Prost and the late Ayrton Senna. From his opening races in Formula One, when he qualified seventh for Jordan Ford, at Spa, and finished fifth for Benetton Ford, at Monza, observers proclaimed the arrival of a rare talent. He celebrated his first anniversary in this, the premier category of the sport, with his maiden victory. In 1994 he became Germany's first world champion and the following season amassed a record-equalling nine race wins in retaining his title and becoming, at the age of 26, Formula One's youngest double champion.

From those early races, however, he has also been accompanied by controversy and acrimony. The switch from Jordan to Benetton provoked a bitter episode of political and legal wrangling. The first Championship would be marred by suspicion, accusations of impropriety, disqualification and suspension; the second, although attained emphatically, still entailed brushes with authority and a continuing conflict, on and off the track, with his main rival, Britain's Damon Hill.

And yet these incidents were little more than irritations compared with the traumatic realisation that Formula One competition could still be fatal. The death of Ayrton Senna, just 24 hours after Roland Ratzenberger was killed, at the 1994 San Marino Grand Prix, made Schumacher agonise over his future. So, too, did Mika Hakkinen's serious accident in practice for the final race of 1995 in Australia.

The experiences, the emotional extremes, have hastened the ageing process, but then those who have known Schumacher well and have worked with him have, to a man, been struck by a maturity and self-assurance beyond his years. Some believe he is not merely confident but arrogant. He, as we shall hear, contends he is professional, serious about his work, and makes no apologies for being ruthless in his endeavours to reach new targets.

Niki Lauda, three times world champion, remarked that Schumacher eliminated most fundamental errors from his driving at a relatively early stage of his Formula One career and that he was, for his age, more advanced than Senna, the driver generally acknowledged as the greatest of his generation.

Alain Prost, who won the Championship four times and a record 51 races, has been similarly impressed. The Frenchman says: 'After only two years in Formula One Michael had to be considered a top driver, not just a young driver without experience. I regarded him more as I regarded Senna. He is always competitive and very rarely does anything silly.

'But it is not only the driver, it is also the man who is important. Outside racing, at testing, for instance, we talked to each other quite a lot, and not only about racing. That kind of relationship is good for drivers in Formula One. He enjoys what he is doing and he lets the public see that. He shows he is happy on the podium and this is something the sport needs.'

Niki Lauda acknowledged Schumacher's talent.

Martin Brundle, one of the sport's most respected figures, partnered Schumacher at Benetton in 1992 and had to come to terms with facts registered by the clock. The Englishman, a former sportscar world champion, says: 'I realised he had a special talent and there was no point blowing my brains out over it. I have felt for some time he is the fastest out there and, even before Senna died, I was convinced that, in terms of raw speed, he was. The guy is awesome. You have to be impressed by his maturity and professionalism. He knows what he wants, where he's going and how to go about it.

'He's also got his feet on the ground. He's refreshingly down to earth and he's got family values. He's close to his parents and does all he can to help his kid brother's racing. I've got a lot of time for him as a person and as a driver, and there's no limit to what he might achieve.'

Others have had less time for Schumacher, as a person, at any rate. Hill, who was involved in a decisive collision with him at the 1994 Australian Grand Prix and tangled with him again during 1995, argues Schumacher flaunts the principles of fair play. He also claims his rival was 'cosseted' by a Benetton team that created an image of their driver disproportionate to his actual ability. Johnny Herbert, another Englishman and Schumacher's team-mate at Benetton in 1995, complained he was made to feel an 'outcast' by comparison with the 'preferential treatment' the German received.

This book attempts not to eulogise but to give a balanced appraisal of Schumacher's career so far. It considers the facts and opinions and presents, for the first time, Schumacher's authorised version of events, providing an exclusive insight into the driver and the man.

Martin Brundle came to terms with his team-mate's speed.

Maiden Grand Prix Victory, Belgium, 1992.

Driven by Fun

Like most of us, Michael Schumacher readily recollects the fun of his childhood. Fun, for this young German, came on four tiny wheels and a seat on a board just a couple of centimetres above the ground, propelled by a buzzing engine at seemingly ludicrous speeds. Little did he know the momentum would carry him through the junior car racing formulae, sportscars and Formula One to become undisputed champion of the world. Little did he care. The young free spirit had all a young free spirit desires.

Which was just as well. The Schumachers were not a wealthy family. Rolf Schumacher, a chimney builder, and his wife, Elisabeth, were a conservative couple who valued traditional principles. They had a modest, two-bedroom flat in Fischenich, near Cologne, and the first of their two sons was born on 3rd January 1969, at a clinic in Hürth-Hermuhlheim. They called him Michael. Ralf would follow some six years later.

Below left Proud parents… Elisabeth and Rolf Schumacher. *Below* Michael outside his mother's snack bar at the Kerpen kart track.

14

The normal boy who found enjoyment driving a go-kart.

The Schumachers moved to a house in the town of Kerpen-Manheim, 40 kilometres away, and it was there that the family were lured into karting. The incident which prompted Rolf Schumacher to take Michael to a go-kart track is now etched in racing folklore. Michael had already had his pedal kart upgraded thanks to his father's resourcefulness. He had transformed the little kart with the installation of an old lawn-mower engine and Michael flexed his instincts for speed on the neighbourhood pavements. That is, until he ran into a lamp-post and his father decided he would be safer on a proper track. So, they travelled the few kilometres along the road to a track at Kerpen-Horrem and Michael became a member of the go-kart club. He was four years old.

'When Michael first had his kart I used to pull him around with a rope,' his father recalls. 'It was normal, just like when we went swimming. Michael could swim before he could walk. I put him in the water when he was a baby and he just paddled away. He trusted me as any son trusts his father. And so when I put the engine in his kart he was happy and never afraid. But when he hit the lamp-post, I realised I had to take him somewhere else.'

Little did Rolf Schumacher realise where that decision would take his boy.

'He had a helmet with an antenna on it, just the same as a cartoon character, and we had to stuff it inside because it was too big for him. It was very funny.'

And fun was all the Schumachers wanted or, indeed, could afford from it.

'We used old parts, anything we could get for Michael's kart. What he always enjoyed most was to drive in the wet, up and down the straight and do hand-brake turns which he soon learned. Even in that first kart, he started drifting, learning how to control it.

Michael got used to handling trophies at an early age... and posing for photographs as German Kart Champion, 1985.

'But it was not only karting that he liked. He was a normal boy and got up to stuff normal boys do: climbing, playing around, other sports. He was never really afraid of anything and everything he did, even then, he did with intensity.'

Karting, however, he did especially well, and even his first injury, sustained at the age of six, did not deter Michael.

'When he had an accident I thought it might make him want to stop. It was quite a bad accident and I told him it was because he had been stupid. I told him never to do it again and made him carry his kart home himself. He did so without a word. It was only when we got home and he took off his clothes that we discovered he had cut his knee and the blood was pouring out. He had it stitched but he didn't complain and he carried on.'

Parental nerves would be examined for another twenty years and more but mother and father, like son, learned to cope with the strain.

'I wouldn't say I have ever really been afraid for Michael, but of course you think about the dangers from time to time,' Rolf Schumacher admits. 'Now, in Formula One, I am always happy when the start is over, because that is the most dangerous point in the race, and after that I just hope he has no technical problems with the car. Yes, you think about what could happen, but it is not so bad. I am not always anxious.

'I didn't imagine in those early days that he would be anything special in karting or car racing, and go on to achieve what he has achieved. No father could imagine something like this of his son. Maybe you wish something like this – but you don't imagine it.'

Young Michael's insatiable appetite for karting involved his parents still more. His father began working on other go-karts at the track and rented them out. Suddenly he had a part-time job, while his wife dispensed 'chips with everything' at the track cafe. Protests from local residents about the noise and general nuisance caused by the kart track forced the club to find a new site, but Michael's course was set.

The fun factor was hugely enhanced by an ability that was soon to distinguish him from the rest. He won races, then the club championship and became something of a celebrity in the area. The first of the column inches were in print.

Michael says: 'I started for the enjoyment, as a hobby, nothing more. It was something I loved. When you are young you do everything. You play football, you play tennis and so on. Toni Schumacher, the German goalkeeper, was a hero of mine and I enjoyed playing football. I still do. I also enjoyed judo, but I decided that was too dangerous!

'In any case, I was best at karting and that was what I enjoyed most. Plus, of course, we were all in this together. My father built my first karts and as I got older I learned to work on the karts and build them myself. The only problem with having my mother there was that I had far too much sausage and chips. I also had too many chocolates in my younger days. These were the things I had to control· when I became professional. Now I eat more sensibly.

'It was good fun just driving around, drifting, sliding and spinning, especially in the wet. I would do 360 degree spins, then I would try 720s, twice round, and all these things. The sport really came to me because I just enjoyed myself.

'At that stage, though, I never thought about becoming a professional racing driver and making a living out of this. I did not think about that until I was 19 or 20. And it was only after Formula Three, when I joined Mercedes, that I thought for certain I could have a future in racing. If I had not become a professional racing driver I would probably still be at the go-kart circuit at Kerpen, like my dad, or teaching young drivers, which was what I did in the later period.'

He was certainly never destined to be an academic. He is patently a bright man, with an alert mind, but studying pained him and further education was not an option he contemplated.

'I finished schooling but I hated school,' he confesses. 'I still hate learning, sitting there, learning the vocabulary of another language. It drives me crazy. At the beginning of 1995, when I was working with Renault, I took French lessons. We did three lessons in one day – three hours. I was going crazy. It was just too much and I could not keep things in my head anymore.

'When it is something I really want to do, or like to do, then it's easy for me. I wanted to learn English because I knew it was the language I had to know in motor racing, so the encouragement came from within myself.

Things I don't like to do, like school, are very difficult for me. When I did my car mechanics' apprenticeship I had to go to school one day a week and I hated this day. I loved to be in the workshop, working on the cars, but I hated the one day at school.'

Even his 'love' of the workshop was evidently a fickle affair. He also says: 'I was never interested in being an engineer, although I realise engineering is such an important part of motor racing. My apprenticeship certainly helped in giving me some understanding and knowledge, but I found it boring. I was never the kind of person who could tune an engine and be very precise. I could not be like a doctor, for instance, who obviously has to be very precise. I could not be the same in terms of engineering.

'But driving was something that did interest me and something in which I felt I could be precise. Here, in a kart and then in a car, I felt I could try to find perfection. I'm not saying I was 100 per cent at all, but it was something I aimed for and which motivated me. It was certainly very helpful to have the knowledge about mechanical aspects, in order to understand the car and how it works, and to be able to explain to the engineers what you expect the car to do. But the real interest – that was driving.'

Schumacher remembers that early mishap in go-karts and confirms it left only physical scars. 'My father told me it was because I was stupid, it was my fault. Now, he said, you can push the go-kart to the garage and it's finished for today or this week or whatever, and I was crying and I pushed it back. We didn't realise I had hurt myself. When I got home, I saw the blood on my knee and had to go to the doctor. But that didn't scare me or make me want to stop. I never scared myself. Even in later years, in more competitive situations, I rarely had accidents. There was only one significant one I can remember. I rolled over and cracked a rib, and that's it. Sure, I had some sore muscles, that sort of thing, but nothing worse than that. I never hurt myself in those days.

'The first time I hurt myself was in Japan, early in my Formula One career, in 1991. It was a big crash in practice, but I got back into the car and went half a second quicker after that. As long as I understand accidents, then it's all right for me.'

(As we shall see, accidents involving other drivers disturbed him deeply and rendered him reluctant to go on until he discovered the cause.)

'In the car I have never actually been scared about having an accident. Even at Imola, where I went off heavily in 1995, when I was sitting in the car and going off the track I just thought "Oh, this is going to hurt". That was all. Then BOOM – and that was it. At that very moment I wasn't afraid that I was going to hurt myself badly.

'If I think back to my school days, then I can well remember the feeling of being afraid. I was scared at school. I once got into a fight and was really afraid, so I said "No", I didn't want to fight and I didn't. That was more scary than anything I experienced in racing. Believe me, I do know the

Boys just wanna have fun.

different between being scared and not being scared.

'At Imola I was totally relaxed, I knew it was going to happen and that I couldn't do anything about it. There wasn't a moment when I thought "Okay, that's it, this sport is too dangerous". But of course, you keep it in mind that it happened at that particular place and you are aware of that the next time round. You want to reach the same limit in the end but you do it bit by bit, and get there a little differently in order to avoid the same thing happening again.

'At Suzuka, when I came to that corner again, I took it a bit easier and wasn't as quick, certainly not flat. And then I developed myself again, and in the end came to the point I had been at before.'

The trials and tribulations of school days perhaps attracted young Michael's attention to an advert propounding the benefits of body-building. Each evening, when classes were over, he would pump weights and exercise, and before very long this mere boy was proudly displaying stomach muscles. His physical condition was to prove a crucial part of his artillery in more serious racing, and even in the 'fun' days he had the commitment to deliver results. But the image of a remorseless automaton is, at best, misleading.

'I was just a normal boy, getting into a little mischief and doing the things everyone does. Girls, discos, all that sort of thing. I had good friends in go-karting. Six of us, all drivers competing in the German Championship, went camping for three weeks and had a lot of good fun. In the evening we went as a group to the disco and I always had to hide behind the others to get in because I was only 12. It was a good time.'

Michael was used to mixing with, competing against and beating older boys – again a taste of things to come. His travels also took him, with his family, to Nivelles, Belgium, in 1980 for the World Kart Championship. One driver, in particular, caught his eye.

'I saw this guy. He was so crazy and yet so impressive the way he drove. I didn't know who he was and the next day I looked in the newspaper to find out. It was Ayrton. After this I followed his career and he became my one idol in motor racing.'

Still younger karting enthusiasts doubtless noted the name of the boy from Kerpen as he rampaged across Germany and Europe during the 1980s, but by then Michael had exhausted the funds of his father and was dependent on a benefactor. Two of his friends in the karting fraternity were the sons of an enthusiast and businessman, Jurgen Dilk, who recognised Michael's talent and his plight. He offered to sponsor Michael and brought other sponsors on board in return for his trophies. The boy racer reckoned he had a good deal.

'My father gave me the possibility to enjoy karting to start with, but after a while the money was not enough. Fortunately, there were other people who will always be important to me, who enabled me to continue. Of course I was lucky to have these people. Without them I would not be here now. It is certainly not normal to have people like these. On the other hand, if I hadn't done the job and satisfied these people with my success, they would not have continued. Some of them were very clever business people.'

So, clearly, was Michael. He also gave them the success they were looking for. Michael was German junior champion in 1984 and retained the title the

Jurgen Dilk, Michael's early sponsor, now runs his fan club.

The inspirational image of Ayrton Senna, 1980.

Double Karting champion, 1987.

following year. That year, too, he was runner-up in the world junior championship at Le Mans. In 1986, after leaving school, he had a professional arrangement which took him to Darmstadt to work in a garage and provided him with a drive alongside the bigger boys in the European championship. He was third in that series and in the domestic championship. Victory at Kerpen launched his triumphant 1987 German championship and he embossed his place in karting by winning the European championship final that year in Gothenburg.

People were already jostling to open doors into car racing for Schumacher, but as yet he had not considered turning his hobby into a career.

'A lot of people were saying I should try this or try that and yes, I was certainly interested in moving on, trying something new. I had won championships in karting and wanted to see what I could do in cars. But it was no more than that. The important thing for me was to continue enjoying my racing. That had always been the important thing and, even now, I enjoy nothing more than going back to my first love, karting. I go back to Kerpen when I can but now I also try to find somewhere nearer my home in Monaco. Just as long as it is a go-kart.'

It was time, though, for another significant change in the life of the young Schumacher, and soon, unbeknown to him, his racing was to become serious business.

Serious Business

Formula Ford and, in Germany, Formula Koenig (an adaptation of the Fiat raced in Italy as Formula Panda) carry the aspirations of young drivers into the arena of car racing. They are small, light cars and look exceedingly fragile. Little more than karts, in fact. But, they are deceptively quick and are genuine single-seater racing cars. Many outstanding kart drivers find the graduation beyond their capabilities. Some may be too set in their ways or lack the gut ambition to prove themselves again. Others simply cannot raise the funds to pursue an ever-more expensive obsession.

Karting, however, is the proven nursery for modern Formula One drivers and Michael Schumacher was to negotiate the next stage of his career with now familiar conviction. His only potential stumbling block was equally familiar – he had no money to buy a drive.

Gustav Hoecker, a Lamborghini dealer in Germany and Formula Koenig entrant, was one of those who monitored Schumacher's progress in 1987 with growing interest. Another was Peter Sieber of the Formula Ford team, EUFRA. Previous discussions with Formula Ford teams had led to nothing because Michael had no cash and the asking price of 500 Deutschmarks threatened to sever this latest contact. Michael called the team and said: 'Sorry, I can't do it because I don't have the money.'

According to those close to Schumacher, an enduring family principle was involved here. Rolf Schumacher did not have loose change to the tune of 500 Deutschmarks and would not go into debt to produce it. A friend says: 'The principle was to spend only what they had and that is the way Michael thinks about money. He is very careful with it. He learned to be sensible about money and now that he is a wealthy man he appreciates what he has. The team owner could not believe this because it was only a symbolic price but eventually said he would give Michael a few laps anyway, and after two or three laps he saw this young guy had talent.'

The theme of the reluctant scholar learning quickly in the fields that inspired him runs through Schumacher's career and life. On the race track he was an attentive pupil and earned the accolade afforded those whose gifts confound the merely good – 'a natural'. The instant acquaintanceship with a Formula Ford 1600 and his subsequent speed at Hockenheim on a bleak day late in 1987 signposted the way.

Opposite above Getting to grips with cars… Formula Koenig, 1988.

Opposite below Making an impression in Formula Ford, 1988.

The following year Schumacher, once again supported by Jurgen Dilk, drove a Van Diemen in Formula Ford competition in Germany and across Europe, and also negotiated a deal with Gustav Hoecker to race his new Formula Koenig car. He was awarded victory in his first race for Hoecker, at Hockenheim, after a disqualification and won many more convincingly on his way to the Formula Koenig championship. He had nine wins from 10 rounds. The Formula Ford Euroseries provided a sterner examination of the young German and he was beaten into second place by another future Formula One driver, Finland's Mika Salo.

It was still an impressive addition to his CV and now the scouts from Formula Three were gathering. Among them was a former driver called Willi Weber, and the reports he collected were confirmed on a wet day in Austria.

'I had a Formula Three team in Germany and always had to look for good young drivers to keep at the top,' Weber says. 'In 1988 I saw a young driver at Salzburg driving Formula Ford 1600 in an excellent way. It was completely impressive for me how this young man handled the car. I didn't know him. All I saw was the number on the car. He left the grid in seventh position and before the first lap was finished he was in front by around seven seconds. I said to myself: this man I need in my Formula Three team.

'I watched him in another two races and then I spoke to him. I asked him if he was interested in driving a Formula Three car. He was completely shocked and asked why him. I replied because you need to show your talent in Formula Three. We made a date for the test and after seven or eight laps Michael was one and a half seconds quicker than my driver, with the same car, so this was the green light for me. This was the man I wanted and I

Schumacher and Willi Weber would have much to celebrate.

immediately offered him a drive for two years. He said he didn't have any money for Formula Three but I told him: I don't need your money, I need your driving. Don't worry about the money, we'll find a way. On the same day we signed the contract and that was the beginning. We have been together ever since.'

Weber intuitively hit the jackpot that day. He became not only Schumacher's Formula Three boss but also his manager on a 10-year contract. Weber was reassured by his young charge's early races in Formula Three, where the competition was distinctly keener. Michael found himself embroiled in a fierce contest with two drivers he had encountered in karts and would become his team-mates further down the road. They were Heinz-Harald Frentzen, a compatriot, and Karl Wendlinger, of Austria.

Schumacher's boss and manager says: 'It was obvious Michael was an extremely good talent in the car because his handling on the limit was so impressive. It was unbelievable and my feeling was completely clear from the first day of Formula Three that we would go together to Formula One. We did not expect it so quickly, but we were well prepared.'

His driver maintains he still had no dreams of Formula One at the outset of his Formula Three campaign. It was a tough environment and, good as he was, he could not presume to have better long term prospects than his main opponents, or those of another front-runner, Michael Bartels. Wendlinger eventually shaded it, becoming German Formula Three champion by one point from both Frentzen and Schumacher.

Weber was content. His protegé had stood up to the test yet still had much to benefit from another year in Formula Three, and the 1990 single-

Schumacher with his Mercedes 'junior' team-mates, Karl Wendlinger and Heinz-Harald Frentzen.

A familiar position, this time in the German Formula Three championship.

seater challenge duly fell into the grand plan. Despite an indifferent opening period, Schumacher ran into a rich vein of form mid-season and took command of the Championship. He won the title by 31 points from Otto Rensing.

Another part of the grand plan involved something completely different and raised eyebrows across Europe. Weber placed Schumacher in the Mercedes sportscar 'academy' alongside Frentzen and Wendlinger. Perceived wisdom in this sport advocates a next move to Formula 3000 for any driver seriously contemplating Formula One, but Weber was sold on the Mercedes junior team scheme, whereby the three young recruits would alternate as partner to the experienced Jochen Mass in one of their cars entered for the World Championship. So, as well as competing in Formula Three, Schumacher would be committed to a programme in the big, powerful Sauber-run 'Silver Arrows'.

Weber recalls, with undisguised satisfaction: 'We made the choice of Mercedes and Group C rather than Formula 3000 and everybody thought me a bad manager. People think that if you drive Group C you are finished, you will never make it back to single-seaters and Formula One. But for Michael it was the right move.'

It was the move which convinced Schumacher he could make a living out of racing – and perhaps even establish himself as a half decent Grand Prix driver.

Schumacher says: 'Right up until this time I still thought of racing as my hobby and it was only after I had done Formula Three and went to Mercedes that I started to think about being professional. Before then I could not be sure about my future at all. I remember, I think in 1989, the first time I discussed with a friend how I would imagine it to be in Formula One. I told him I thought that if I could drive somewhere in the mid-field, that would be great. But that was it, just casually talking, dreaming.'

The reality of the sportscar environment hit Schumacher forcibly. The three juniors were summoned by their Mercedes 'headmaster', Jochen Neerpasch, to their first test at the Paul Ricard circuit, in the south of France, where they met up with their tutor, Jochen Mass.

'It was clear straightaway that we were competing against each other,' Schumacher says. 'I well remember our first five laps. We all had to do five laps, in turn. I think I was the last of the three. Wendlinger started, Frentzen went second. Jochen [Mass] went in front of us to set up the car, principally.

'I went out on to the circuit to watch the others and when I listened how they used the throttle I thought this turbo-charged engine seems to be very difficult. They seemed scared to put down the throttle because if the turbo came in and made a big push, especially with the car being very critical, and you get wheel-spin, you could go off immediately. I was very afraid of this happening.

'I think Wendlinger did a one minute 11 something after his five laps, then Heinz-Harald, I think, a 1:6.8, and I did a 1:6.4. Everybody says Heinz-Harald was the quickest out of the three in the first test, which was not quite the case. These, I believe, were the times after the first five laps and at the end of the test I think I was still the quickest, although I am not 100 per cent sure. I believe Karl was two or three seconds behind us and Heinz-Harald and I were quite close together.

'Heinz-Harald was very good was when we went to Jerez to test. We were asked to simulate a race distance, taking stints in turn. We had to drive within the fuel limit and make the best lap times possible. Karl started and used too much fuel, and when I went out I achieved good times but was over the fuel limit. Heinz-Harald went out and was really fast, but within the fuel limit. I could not believe it when the team told me how much fuel he had used.

'When he went out again I listened how he was driving and I understood it. So, on my second 30-lap stint I drove in the same smooth, consistent way and was able to do exactly the same – still fast but within the fuel limit. It is a different style of driving – the way I drove at the 1994 Spanish Grand Prix when I finished with only fifth gear. A lot of people say that he was better than me, so I would just like to clear up those first impressions. After that, I think the results speak for themselves.'

Competitive instincts are always liable to expose sensitivities, even among the best of friends. The junior trio developed a close relationship. They worked together and played together. Frentzen has recently expressed an opinion that Schumacher had been too competitive in what should have been lighter moments, but in the interim their relationship had changed. Not surprisingly, considering Schumacher took up with and then married Frentzen's former girlfriend, Corinna Betsch.

Frentzen, nearly two years older than Schumacher – a factor often overlooked when their early performances are compared – said: 'Michael had to win no matter what we were doing. Even if we had a game of pool, he had to win. He could not play just for the fun of it, which was what I wanted to do.'

Schumacher, irked by the comment, confronted Frentzen. 'I told him he should not say this sort of thing because it is not correct. Heinz-Harald was always a person who enjoyed life. He enjoyed wine, good food and so on, and the word "serious", especially at this time, didn't exist for him. He didn't train, he didn't have discipline. But I did, and that's why, for him, it looked as if I was very serious. When we played pool I wanted to win, but I didn't go crazy if I didn't win. If you play any sport, of course you try to win.

'I think Heinz-Harald knows himself that he has improved a lot in this area. He is very different to what he used to be. When we went to the gym together I would say "Okay, let's have half an hour on the bicycle", he would say "Aagh, ten minutes is enough". But I enjoyed the time with him. We had great times together, and I'm sure he learned that training was more important than he had thought.

'We trained quite a lot together and I remember the first time we went to Willi Dungl's [a much-vaunted sports treatment and training clinic in Austria]. We were put through the Cooper test, which means running with a coach for a maximum of 12 minutes and achieving as great a distance as you can. I managed to stay about 20 or 30 metres behind him and was quite happy with this. When Heinz-Harald ran he had to stop after seven minutes as he was out of breath and said "No, I can't do any more".

'For me this was competition. I wanted to be as good as I could be and, even though I went over my limit, I made it. When we did push-ups, I did the maximum number, but for Heinz-Harald, it was not important. But we were good friends and saw a lot of each other as he lived only 40 kilometres from me.

'I didn't see Karl so much away from racing because he lived in Austria. When we were together he was always the quietest of the three and was difficult to have a conversation with. You always had to start the conversation and most of the time he would just say "Yes" or "No". You couldn't really get close to him. He had his friends and with them he opened up and became free. And if there was a good-looking girl, then his mouth would never stop. Heinz-Harald and I were always laughing about this. Suddenly you would see him, alone, with a girl, chatting like he never wanted to stop and we would say "It's not possible". That was Karl.'

Mixing with the senior drivers, Mass and the pair who shared the lead car, Jean-Louis Schlesser and Mauro Baldi, was an important part of the curriculum devised by Neerpasch and accommodated by the team boss, Peter Sauber. Schumacher says: 'Jochen Mass was always important when you had questions – how to do things, where to go. He had the experience, told you how and gave you directions. It was up to you whether you took the directions. We often had dinner together as a group, the three of us with Jochen, Jean-Louis, Mauro and sometimes Peter Sauber. This also helped my English develop because if I, or one of the others, didn't know a word, Jochen explained to us.'

The education was wide-ranging. 'We learned very quickly what we should do and should not do, what was important and what was not important through the school at Mercedes. It was not a school in the way that people outside perhaps imagine – it was just that we talked about things. Neerpasch was good at this. He gave us a very good direction.'

It is well chronicled that Neerpasch gave Schumacher a paternal lecture on what was and what was not expected of a Mercedes factory driver after his student was stopped for speeding and had his car confiscated by French police en route to a test at Paul Ricard. Schumacher – as we have seen, a proud man and a stickler for accuracy – paints the scene in a different tone.

Serious talking… with Jochen Neerpasch (*left*) and Peter Sauber.

Schumacher with his 'senior' Mercedes drivers, Jochen Mass (*left*) and Jean-Louis Schlesser.

'I did not have to be told,' he says. 'I knew myself that this was not something acceptable. I had been told about the way to behave, the public image and all that sort of thing, but not because of this particular incident. I knew myself what was right.'

Above all, he wanted to learn about the car, the circuit and racing. 'These were the things I learned quickly because I had the interest to learn about them.'

The learning process would involve some harsh lessons and he fell foul of officialdom at Silverstone in a forerunner of controversy to come. He was scheduled to make his debut in the World Sportscar Championship but his car was excluded for work done 'outside' the pits and he was disqualified for driving with his seatbelts undone, a charge he strenuously disputed.

The prestigious end-of-season Macau Formula Three race provided another glimpse of Formula One things to come. Schumacher, who retired from the event the previous year, lost the first heat in 1990 to Mika Hakkinen and the Finn had only to stay on the German's heels in the second heat to take first prize. Instead he tried to overtake, Schumacher closed the door and Hakkinen crashed out. Victory at Fuji completed a Far East double for Schumacher and capped his Formula Three campaign.

Nothing more to be achieved in Formula Three, Schumacher focused on sportscars for 1991. He partnered Wendlinger, while Mass joined Schlesser in the champions' line-up. Frentzen opted for the Formula 3000 route.

Silver Arrow in flight...
Schumacher at Le Mans, 1991.

Retirements at Suzuka and Monza and second place at Silverstone brought Schumacher and company to Le Mans and the 24-hour classic. Schumacher, reeling off a series of fast laps, was well pleased with himself. Older heads in the camp, including Mass, were not so impressed and the tutor delivered another lecture.

'Jochen said to me "Why are you going so fast?". I said "Sorry, I don't use the brakes, I don't use the gearbox, I don't use the tyres, I don't use the fuel. I can be quick without giving the car a hard time". In fact, I well remember Jonathan Palmer [another driver] looking at my times and then my fuel consumption, and being so surprised because if he got close to my times he'd use twice the amount of fuel.

'Now I have to say that Jochen was right because there were circumstances we didn't know about at the time. We had a boost button, which was mainly for qualifying and overtaking, and I asked the Mercedes people whether I could use it if I was within the fuel limit. They said I could and I used it on the straights in this stint in the night, when I made the fastest lap. The other drivers did the same but suddenly we got higher water temperatures and the cylinder seal went because there was too much pressure. That had not been tested on the car.

'Then we got a gearbox problem, when Karl was driving during the night. He was stuck in fourth gear but I'm not sure whether this was because I went so quickly, because something broke, or because Karl had a bad shift. I felt I

Master of Macau.

had given it really easy selection. I do agree now that it wasn't necessary to go five or ten seconds quicker than the rest. I could have gone just one or two seconds faster. Having said that, ours was the only car from the team to finish.'

Fifth place, however, was scant consolation. There would be better and more dramatic days ahead for Schumacher. And not very far ahead.

The conviction that sportscars were the way to go did not totally close Schumacher's eyes to Formula 3000. He went to Japan for one race and finished second. He returned to the Mercedes at the Nurburgring but had to retire the sick car. It was during this weekend that Weber sensed the opportunity to manoeuvre his driver into Formula One. Jordan Ford would

Top right Mika Hakkinen lost his chance at Macau.

Victory at Fuji completes an uplifting double.

be seeking a replacement for Bertrand Gachot, who had been jailed in England for spraying gas in the face of a taxi driver. The next Grand Prix was just a week later, at Belgium's Spa-Francorchamps circuit.

Weber says: 'I heard on the Saturday that Gachot was in jail and I thought this was my chance, I would try to get Michael in this one race, to show his talent. The Jordan car was a fantastic one at the time, and of course I knew what Michael could do. I knew Eddie Jordan from Formula Three, called him up and told him I had the man for him. He said "Who the hell is Schumacher?" I told him but he said "Oh, Willi, come on". I kept on at him and in the end we did a deal.'

Jordan, of course, knew very well who Schumacher was. As a Formula One boss it is his job to be aware of rising talent. But he was in a position of strength, he had something Schumacher and Weber wanted, and business is business. And when it came to business, Dubliner Jordan was acknowledged as a canny operator. Even if Schumacher satisfied him in the test, at Silverstone, he would have to pay for the race. Weber was undeterred.

Diplomacy was required to assuage Mercedes and eventually Neerpasch played a prominent role in shaping Schumacher's Formula One career. The test having earned Schumacher rave reviews inside the Jordan camp, his Grand Prix debut was secured. Mercedes agreed to pick up the bill by way of investment, insisting on a clause in any subsequent long term contract giving them the right to reclaim Schumacher should their Formula One plans run to schedule. Schumacher still had racing commitments with Sauber Mercedes that season and would complete his sportscar racing with victory at the Japanese circuit, Autopolis. From now on, however, he would be known as a Formula One driver. And soon, a very well known Formula One driver.'

'It is fair to say joining Mercedes was a gamble for me, but in the end it was not a gamble at all,' he now says. 'It was a gamble to decide on this direction, but I chose the right direction. Mercedes was certainly a key landmark in my career. At the same time, I have always made the right decision at the right time. I made the decision to go to Mercedes rather than into Formula 3000 and it was correct. I did race in 3000, but I made the decision to go to Japan and do one race instead of two. The right decision now was to try Formula One.'

The proud man, the stickler for accuracy. We shall see more of that.

Schumacher completes his sportscar racing with victory at Autopolis, Japan, 1991.

34

Formula One Calls

In the late summer of 1991, Michael Schumacher, already recognised as a quick learner, had much learning to do, and very quickly. For a start, he had to find his way to the Belgian Grand Prix circuit of Spa-Francorchamps. Situated just over the border with Germany and in fact, closer to his home in Kerpen than Hockenheim, it was still unchartered territory for the 22-year-old. He got lost on the way and had to ring back to base for further directions. Had Eddie Jordan been aware of his near misadventure he might have pulled out of the deal.

That option did occur to Jordan later that Thursday when, to his horror, he discovered his new driver had never raced at the track. All circuits are different, all have their own characteristics and all impose their own demands. Spa happens to be more different than most. A combination of public road and purpose-built sections cuts a swathe through the forests of the Ardennes. Few dispute it is the most beautiful circuit in Formula One. It is also the longest and most daunting. The scenic splendour cloaks some of

Brief encounter... Eddie Jordan and the starlet who left him.

The debut that amazed Formula One. Schumacher qualifies seventh for the 1991 Belgian Grand Prix.

the fastest corners on the tour and the capricious weather, deep into August, confronts drivers with ever-changing hazards.

Jordan, then in his first season of Formula One but a successful team boss in the lower formulae, still winces as he recalls: 'I couldn't believe it when he said he'd never been round the place before. It was just automatic to think he would have been to Spa. He lived only 50 miles or so from there. It turned me off and I thought he wouldn't qualify.'

The most serious threat to Schumacher's debut, however, was a contractual dispute that would rumble on for the next fortnight, erupt at Monza, and rumble on again for some years afterwards, as Jordan pursued the matter in the courts. That Thursday afternoon and evening, Jordan sought a binding, long-term commitment from Schumacher, whose advisers recommended caution.

Jordan says: 'At that stage I'd told him he wasn't driving and I'd rung Stefan Johansson (a Swede with considerable Formula One experience) to say come along. He was on his way, which was a little embarrassing, but I was not prepared to race Schumacher until he was quite clear I had the rights and the option over his services for three years, because I was taking a big chance. I didn't want to bring him into Formula One, find he was good and suddenly he's gone. There would be no logic in that.'

'There was a fee, which Mercedes agreed – £150,000 for the race but there was no fee for the test. The payment came from Mercedes and there was a guarantee of three years on this payment because Mercedes were looking to bring this guy on and we were the best school in the world. The only stipulation was that if Mercedes themselves came into Formula One they would have call on him, which I accepted.'

Precisely what Schumacher, represented by Neerpasch and Weber, accepted is at issue. Whatever the contents of the 'letter of intent' or 'pre-contract' – and it is acknowledged by both parties that a document affirming Schumacher's intention to sign a contract was amended by the driver's camp – it was agreed the German would race the Jordan at Spa and the contract in respect of further Grands Prix would be attended to after the Belgian event.

Jordan says: 'His lawyers, probably quite sharply, said "Oh no, it's too difficult to go through all this contract in the middle of the race meeting". There are no doubts.'

Schumacher says: 'At that moment I said I couldn't sign. First of all, I could not read and understand well enough what it said and secondly, I didn't know what was in the other contract, so how could I sign it? And then it was quite critical because I felt Eddie forced me to sign, otherwise somebody else would have got the car the next day. I said I could not sign until I had spoken to Mr Neerpasch, or someone who could help me in this matter. Finally, Jochen read through it and said "Change these two words and you are going to be fine". That's what we did and I signed a letter which said I was going to sign "in agreement" rather than "the agreement", which says that in agreement we are going to agree. But we never agreed this agreement.'

Meanwhile, Michael had more learning on the agenda. He jumped onto a bike and, for the first time, went round the spectacular, climbing, plunging, meandering 6.94 km (4.312 mile) circuit. 'I found out about the circuit for myself, riding my bicycle. It was normal,' he says in his disarmingly simplistic way. The next morning he would go round again, this time in a Grand Prix racing car.

For all the anxieties and the hassles, Jordan, who enjoys his fame as a team owner bold enough to give youth its fling, was content to have Schumacher in his car on that Friday, 23rd August 1991.

'I felt he could do it but this was before he had done anything dramatic,' Jordan says. 'At this stage people were seriously struggling to spell his name properly. People were telling me this was a major risk, straight out of sportscars, never been done before – crazy. We were a young team but this, we were told, was madness.

'But Trevor Foster, our team manager at the time, had seen straightaway in that test that he was obviously dynamic. We'd had our Alesis, Herberts, Irvines, Frentzens and Hills, and a whole lot of others in Formula 3000, but you could see immediately that he was in a different class and the closest we'd seen to Senna, who had tested for us in Formula Three, in 1982. That

Now you see him… Colleagues for a race, Trevor Foster *(left)* and Andrea de Cesaris.

was mindblowing, and this was equally mindblowing.'

Foster's assessment was confirmed during that first practice session at Spa. Jordan and his staff observed the new man with near disbelief as his lap times came down.

'Nick Burrows, the number one mechanic on that car who had been with us for a long time and worked with all these other good drivers, put him in the car. When the car came in and we saw the time, he looked over his glasses at me and I glanced at him. Not a word was spoken. He had a little smirk on his face that said "We've dialled into a gem here". And during the session, that became more and more evident.'

So much so that the arrival of Michael Schumacher became the talk of Formula One that weekend. He lined up for his Formula One debut seventh on the grid. His team-mate, the vastly experienced Italian, Andrea de Cesaris, was fourteenth. Sometimes, very occasionally, sport brings us an individual of such sublime talent you just know he or she is a star in the making. Some say they saw it in George Best on the day he made his debut for Manchester United. Others contend it was obvious only in his second appearance, three months later. Schumacher's first weekend can have left no-one in doubt.

His first race, alas, was a huge disappointment. His clutch burnt out virtually from the start and he rolled to a halt. His influence, however, had a more prolonged effect.

'It fired up de Cesaris,' Jordan relates. 'With two laps to go he was in second place, catching Senna, who had a problem, and the engine let go. All eyes were on Schumacher but in the race de Cesaris drove like a demon.'

Schumacher was driving into a major row. Although he again tested the Jordan Ford at Silverstone after the Belgian Grand Prix and was due to sign a contract with the team, moves were afoot to switch him to Benetton Ford before the next race in Italy. Schumacher's backers and management – augmented by the specialist international company, IMG – were said to be unhappy with certain aspects of the Jordan proposal and maintained there was no binding agreement with the Silverstone-based team.

Schumacher says evidence of Jordan's intention to change to Yahama engines the following year swayed the decision to join Benetton. 'We had understood that Jordan would continue with a Ford engine and then we learned about their plans to go with Yamaha, which was why we changed our minds. Jochen Neerpasch was very important at this time and persuaded me

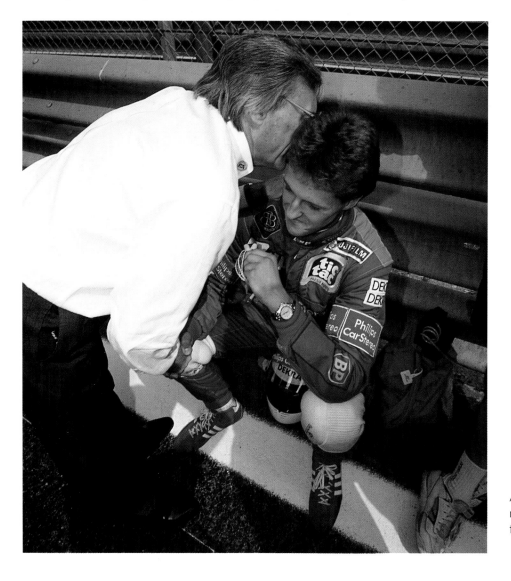

A word in your ear, son. The new boy soon gets the message from Bernie Ecclestone at Spa, 1991.

Roberto Moreno leaves
Benetton to make way for
Schumacher.

to go in this direction. I well remember, after that second test at Silverstone, sitting for one and a half hours with Trevor Foster, discussing the Yamaha engines. I said this engine was so heavy, not enough power, it could not be the right way to go. He tried to persuade me it would work, but I felt it would not take me in the direction I wanted.'

Jordan: 'Yamaha was never mentioned in the contract but at that stage it was a perfectly legitimate thing to do. It was a works engine, paid for by the factory, with all the support and technology behind it. Ford was a £3 million a year deal, Benetton had the factory engine and we were the support to that. I wanted to be out of the support bracket.'

Schumacher: 'I really wanted to finish the season with them, and then maybe change, but it wasn't possible. I had to make the decision, either now or not, and, faced with a situation like this, where you have the possibility of going to Benetton knowing you can continue to go forward there, or going into the unknown, then it's a bit easier to reach that decision.'

Assured Schumacher was a free agent, Benetton signed him and sacked their number two driver, the Brazilian, Roberto Moreno. Jordan went to the High Court in an attempt to block Schumacher's move but his application failed. It was Thursday, 5th September, the day before first practice at Monza. That evening, in Milan, Moreno successfully sought an injunction preventing anyone but himself from driving the Benetton. It meant this increasingly messy business was back on Formula One's doorstep and, as usually happens in these situations, Bernie Ecclestone, president of the Formula One Constructors' Association, vice-president (marketing) of FIA, motor sport's governing body, and omnipotent broker, swept into action. His court was the sumptuous Villa d'Este hotel on Lake Como.

'When Benetton heard the verdict from Milan they were suicidal,' Jordan says. 'I got a message from Bernie asking us to go to the Villa d'Este. Flavio Briatore and Tom Walkinshaw from Benetton were there, plus Weber and Schumacher. There were helicopters and lawyers flying about and it was getting heated. I refused to take any money. I told Bernie and Flavio we were not going to be bought off with a fistful of gold. In the end the way out was a $500,000 settlement for Moreno.'

By then the subject of this extraordinary, high-powered wrangle, was oblivious to everything. 'Bernie said "Go to bed, we'll sort it out". Then he called me at one or two o'clock in the morning, expecting me to be sitting there, waiting for the call and being nervous about whether or not I would be driving the following morning, but I was actually in a deep, deep sleep. However, it was a big relief when it was all over.'

As well as his half million, Moreno was given the Jordan drive, but there was little by way of consolation for his new boss. He had lost his gem and, in the early hours of the morning, was miles from his hotel. He was offered a bed at the Villa d'Este – as long as he was prepared to share it with his marketing man, Ian Phillips!

Jordan says: 'I'd had enough after the carry-on at the Villa d'Este. I'd never known anything like it. But we are suing over the matter and Michael has to respond. The crux of the litigation is the clear German letter, and they don't deny it was altered. It's for a judge to decide whether it was normal business practice, foul play, opportunism or downright deceitfulness. I don't really have a problem with Michael. I can see he was heavily steered. It's only recently that he's been able to look me in the eye again. But I don't feel it should become a personal issue.'

The sense of opportunity lost still gnaws at the Irishman. 'I know there is an argument that Michael was better off at Benetton, but they were then in a similar position to where Jordan are now, and had he stayed for the three years Jordan would have been in a far better position than they are now. We knew what we had.'

And yet even when he knew he had Schumacher no more, Jordan was able to laugh at himself. 'The joke in the team is that we've got to get better hotels to keep our drivers. The place we had that weekend at Spa was a school or a borstal and we were sleeping in dormitories. It was the worst hotel we've ever had in Formula One. So Michael goes from that to the Villa d'Este – no wonder he signed for Benetton!'

Jordan adds: 'He's not really developed better than I expected. We'd had Frentzen the year before, in Formula 3000, and he was quick, but Schuey was a much more confident person. Frentzen seems to be shying away from the killer punch. Instead of being at Sauber he should be somewhere like Williams, taking on these big guys. Schumacher hits it straight on, which you have to respect. What did surprise me was when he left Benetton, but I don't think he'd have done that without interference from management.

'The more Michael has gone on, the more like Senna he has become, although he does not yet have the presence Senna had. When you are the champion of your sport I think you have to take on an ambassadorial role, and Senna did that with dignity and style. Michael seems to be more reclusive. He isn't close to many people in the paddock because he's very serious and focused. However, I am one of Michael's biggest fans. Why shouldn't I be? We were responsible for finding him.

'One good thing that has come out of it all is the Contracts Recognition Board, a decisive and organised framework that has since dealt with a number of similar issues and seems to be working extraordinarily well.'

What came out of it for Schumacher was an alliance that took on and ultimately beat the world. He says: 'I have to admit I have been lucky, otherwise I wouldn't be in the position I am in now. Maybe it would have been the same for me as it has been for Rubens Barrichello, still at Jordan and, after three years, still waiting for his first win.

'It was a difficult decision to leave Jordan because they were good at that time, I was very happy to get the chance of my first race with them and I felt a little bound to them because of this, not because of the controversial issues.

I did not feel 100 per cent comfortable with the move because for the first race they gave me a good service and I didn't know anything about Formula One until I went there.

'Eddie is still chasing me for this, to get some money and, although Eddie is known as a man who gives young drivers a chance, he is also a man who knows how to do business. Do not misunderstand me. I am not suggesting he is a bad person and do not want it to sound like that. I will always be grateful that he gave me the chance. But I think it has been proved it was the right decision for me and Eddie was paid for the drive, so he certainly made something out of it.'

Jordan's partnership with Yamaha lasted one season. The team tumbled from fifth in the 1991 Constructors' Championship to joint eleventh in 1992.

On that Friday morning at Monza, in 1991, Schumacher went about his work almost as if nothing had happened, as if he had been a Benetton driver

Schumacher hounds Ferrari's Alain Prost at Monza in 1991, but this champion resists.

all season. What had happened upset not only Moreno but also two other Brazilian drivers. Senna deemed the removal of his compatriot 'not correct' and the undercurrent of resentment would be evident in his relations with Schumacher. Perhaps even more embittered was Nelson Piquet, the driver of the other Benetton and now reluctant team-mate of the young German.

Piquet, a triple champion, had immediate cause for concern. Schumacher qualified seventh for the Italian Grand Prix, Piquet eighth. In the race, Schumacher, scoring his first two Championship points, was fifth, Piquet sixth. In Portugal their race positions were reversed and another sixth place in Spain gave the new boy a third consecutive finish in the points. A crash in practice for the Japanese Grand Prix and retirements in the race there and in Australia tempered the clamour surrounding Schumacher, but Benetton were content that their judgement was sound. Piquet doubtless feared as much, too. A great champion, caught up by the passage of time and the advance of the irresistible tyro, left Benetton and Formula One at the end of the season.

Schumacher says: 'When I went to Benetton I could not have imagined what would happen. I only knew that I could be as I was with Jordan. I have never set myself targets that were too high and I did not when I joined Benetton. I lived for the moment and I was satisfied with the results our maximum effort could achieve. For us there was, realistically, no better place than sixth or seventh because of Williams, McLaren and Ferrari. They were just in front of us. If they had problems or we were at a circuit that was good for our car, we could change the picture a little. But as long as we fulfilled realistic expectations I had reason to be happy.

'It certainly surprised me that I was able to do well straightaway in Formula One. You go into this strange new world, you expect nothing exceptional, you try to be realistic, and suddenly...

'I went to Benetton expecting to be number two to Piquet and that was my target. I said to myself that if I can be within a certain time of him I can be satisfied. Back to my first thought of Formula One: if I could run in the middle of the field, fantastic. Then, when I came into Formula One, I was quicker than de Cesaris. I just couldn't believe this.

'Even then, though, I did not set my targets higher. I always have a personal feeling of where the limit is, and I try to reach it. I didn't achieve it all the time as I was not as consistent then as I am now. But that was what I sought, to find the limit of the car, and when I achieved that I knew it was the maximum. I tried different ways of achieving that, of going quicker, but I never attempted to go over the limit. I knew the car had a limit and that was it.

'Personally, I have a different limit. If the car goes quicker, I can go quicker, and I have never felt I have reached the personal limit, where I couldn't possibly go any quicker. It has always been the limit of the car.

'I never saw other drivers as targets for me to aim at. I never wanted to become an Ayrton Senna or an Alain Prost. I have always wanted only to be myself. I have never dreamed of being a different person. For some reason,

The sparkling German puts his team-mate Nelson Piquet in the shade at Barcelona, 1991.

though, I knew from the first Grand Prix I finished at Monza, that I could compete with these guys. I was driving behind Prost and, in fact, was quicker than him. He made a mistake and I tried to pass him, but it wasn't quite enough.

'People ask me whether I thought these guys were normal human beings or whether they were supermen. From the outside this is something you do not know because you get the impression they are supermen, that they are racing in a different world. I certainly wondered whether or not I could fight and compete against them, and the question was answered for me at Monza. I realised then that they were normal human beings. If you think about it, they do all the things the rest of us do. No, they are not supermen.'

The gathering momentum.

Human emotions were predictably racked when Schumacher moved in alongside Piquet at Benetton. Michael says: 'I had heard all about drivers in Formula One not talking to their team-mates, so I expected it to be a very difficult situation between us. I was open straightaway, talking about what the car was doing, saying how I wanted the car, that I felt we should do this or that, and asking what the others felt. Nelson was the one who just listened. He never talked while I was in the meetings or de-briefings. When I went out, he started talking to his engineer. I know that.

'I said to myself "Okay, triple world champion, if that's the way he wants to be, let him". It didn't disappoint me. I expected it, to be honest. It didn't affect me because I was quicker than him, which was the main reason why he was like that. I knew it was difficult for him, that he tried to hide and didn't want to work with me, but for me that was not a problem. When you are quicker you have no problem with situations like this. You have more confidence.

'The important thing for me was that I was certain I had again made the correct move in going to Benetton. Way back in go-karts, through my early years racing and now in the first part of my Formula One career, I somehow made the right decision at the right time. I suppose it is partly instinct, but I try to steer the instinct with the facts and I have always been prepared to consider the facts that were there. The facts steered me in this direction.'

Opposite The confident look of a future champion.

Crowning Glories

The next four years were to confirm Michael Schumacher's instincts and calculations were as reliable in the rarified atmosphere of Formula One as they had been down at the local kart track, jostling with his chums. The rise and rise of the young German and his Anglo-Italian team was the stuff of celluloid fantasies. A drama of success and controversy would be played out against a backdrop of tension and tragedy.

Martin Brundle replaced Nelson Piquet as Schumacher's team-mate and openly challenged the aspirations of the 23-year-old with just a handful of Grand Prix appearances to his name. Brundle, a mature, respected Englishman, had taken Ayrton Senna to the wire in the 1983 British Formula Three Championship, and won the World Sportscar Championship and the Le Mans 24-Hour race during his exiles from Formula One, but felt unfulfilled in the Grand Prix arena. Benetton Ford, he sensed, would provide him with the opportunity to force that elusive breakthrough and no upstart from across the water was going to interfere with his plans. Four races into the 1992 season Brundle, also an intelligent, well-adjusted man, abandoned his attempt to prove he could out-pace his team-mate.

'I realised he was an exceptional talent and there was no point in blowing my brains out over it,' Brundle recalls. 'Anyone would struggle to keep up with him.'

That psychological burden removed, Brundle in fact kept in touch with Schumacher's scoring rate for the rest of the season. After the blanks of the first quarter, he registered points in 11 of the remaining 12 races and the one that got away, in Canada, would probably have been the big one, the elusive win. That had to be the day his car failed him – the story of Brundle's Formula One life. The last page of his Benetton chapter had been written long before he hauled in his catch of results. He would lose his seat in 1993 to the veteran Italian, Riccardo Patrese.

Schumacher was among those sorry to see Brundle depart. They had developed a productive partnership, the experienced pro willingly imparting his knowledge and the rapidly developing novice gratefully absorbing it. Brundle drew satisfaction from his 'big brotherly' influence and was to retain a fraternal interest and pride in Schumacher's progress long after they parted.

The controversial debut for Benetton at Monza, 1991.

Brundle reflects: 'I've had some epic fights over the years with Senna and Schumacher. They hit you hard and they drive you on. That's always been my strong point, my determination. I've never been as naturally gifted as Senna and Schumacher and that's a fact. I don't delude myself. But let's be honest, who in the last 10 or 15 years has been?'

Schumacher's gift became more apparent with every race. By stark contrast with Brundle, he trawled points from the first four Grands Prix of 1992, standing on the podium on three occasions and exhibiting a fresh, unfettered joy that symbolised his arrival as a challenger to the old order. Again unlike Brundle, he was to land the big one, and the separating destinies of their careers were to be defined on that fateful day at Spa, the very circuit where Schumacher had made his Formula One debut.

Spa is Schumacher's favourite circuit, just about every driver's favourite circuit with its natural, dramatic contours, its awesome high-speed corners, its capriciously changing conditions; at once intimidating and inspiring, cruel and rewarding; the ultimate driving test. Schumacher responded to its demands as the gifted do. Eau Rouge, the most feared, revered and fabled of its demands, at a 180 mph plunge down the hill, flick left and right and back

up the hill at the other side, was to be confronted with relish. And taken flat. 'It is such a natural circuit that it gives you so much satisfaction when you drive it well,' Schumacher says. 'The fast corners, like Eau Rouge, are very tricky.'

'Very tricky' to you and me is terrifying, but then these people do not talk of courage. Of course they are brave, it is just that they do not see bravery as an element. Stirling Moss, one of the greatest drivers of all time, consistently maintains: 'Bravery is one step from stupidity.' However much they tell themselves they are driving within their limits, the fact remains that accidents will happen and, at fast circuits like Spa, the consequences are more likely to be catastrophic. In recent seasons Gerhard Berger, going down the hill into Eau Rouge, and Alessandro Zanardi, coming up the other side, have been particularly fortunate. The big German hope before Schumacher, Stefan Bellof, was not. He died in a sportscar race in 1985.

Conditions at the 1992 Belgian Grand Prix were, to coin Schumacher's phrase, 'very tricky'. The rains came and went, the track glistened then dried. Tactics and tyre choice would be critical. Even so, the odds favoured a familiar scenario. Nigel Mansell and his Williams Renault had dominated the season and the 39-year-old Englishman had been crowned champion after the previous race in Hungary. One of his more anxious afternoons had been in Spain, where one driver had threatened to close in through the rain. In the end Mansell was able to respond, but the young Schumacher had made his impression on the old lion.

At Spa the normally reliable Williams faltered and teased Mansell as much as the weather did. Senna, normally a master in these circumstances, gambled on staying with slicks in the downpour and for once his hunch was wrong. The door opened up for Benetton. Brundle barged through it when Schumacher made a mistake and went wide at Stavelot, but here was destiny's crossroads. Schumacher noticed his partner's tyres were blistered and went in immediately for slicks. By the time the rest had changed, the driver with one year's experience in Formula One was in command.

The 'old head on young shoulders' that Brundle repeatedly referred to would outwit all-comers in the campaigns beyond. But for now he was content to lose his head in delirious celebration. If standing on the podium at his first German Grand Prix had brought a tear to his eye, this maiden victory demanded he cry unashamedly. And he did.

Schumacher completed his first full season in Formula One third in the Championship, just three points behind Patrese, in the other Williams, and most satisfyingly, three ahead of Senna. And herein lay the subplot that now fascinated all Formula One and would emerge as the sport's central issue: did Senna, acknowledged as the pre-eminent driver of the time, have a genuine rival?

Taking the plunge with the Ferrari at Eau Rouge, Spa, 1996.

The potential challenge had manifested itself not only in Schumacher's driving but also in his demeanour and body language. It was evident almost straightaway: a strut if not a swagger, a self-assurance if not an arrogance. Then, to gasps of disbelief at a press conference following the Brazilian Grand Prix in Sao Paulo, Senna's home city, the rookie admonished The Great One for 'playing a game' by slowing in the corners and accelerating on the straights, so preventing him from overtaking.

Senna later explained he had an intermittent engine cut-out problem and suggested the newcomer to Formula One should check the facts before criticising another driver. Sound advice, which Schumacher duly acknowledged, but he had ruffled Senna's feathers and there was more ruffling to come.

In the French Grand Prix, at Magny-Cours, Schumacher was over-ambitious in his attempt to take Senna into the hairpin and the Brazilian was punted out of the race. Schumacher continued after repairs and was on the grid for the restart following a break enforced by heavy rain when Senna, having changed into his civvies, confronted him. The three-times world champion remonstrated with Schumacher over the collision and made the point that he preferred to deliver his views directly, not through the media. Cool as Schumacher endeavours to remain at all times, he did not appreciate the lecture minutes before the resumption of racing and was to be involved

Closing on Mansell at the 1992 Spanish Grand Prix.

Mansell's tribute to the local hero, Hockenheim, 1992.

in another clash, this time with Stefano Modena, and this time the Benetton driver retired.

The acrimony bubbled over later that summer at a test session on the German Grand Prix circuit, Hockenheim. Senna, incensed Schumacher had brake-tested him, climbed from his car and made for the Benetton camp. He grabbed Schumacher by the throat and had to be dragged away by his own McLaren mechanics, who sensed the objective of their driver's mission. Schumacher attempted to laugh off the incident, surmising a massage was on offer.

Observers perceived a deliberate campaign by Schumacher to undermine the very man he had idolized. He was adamant he had merely admired Senna, that the Brazilian had never been his idol. Schumacher now feels able to tell us, in this book, that Senna was his idol. His only idol.

Whatever the contradictions, it was clear Senna had an authentic rival. They had another coming together in the opening race of the 1993 Championship, in South Africa. Schumacher went out, Senna went on to finish second, behind the Williams now in the hands of Alain Prost following Mansell's defection to IndyCars.

Formula One braced itself for a running feud between Senna and Schumacher, especially as their teams were involved in a political squabble over engines. McLaren, having lost Honda, changed to Ford, who were

Victory out of the blue – Estoril, 1993.

committed to giving Benetton priority. Frustrated at being squeezed out of the Williams equation by Prost and uncertain of McLaren's competitiveness, Senna agreed only to a race-by-race contract.

Senna, triumphant in Brazil, was at his beguiling best in a wet Grand Prix of Europe at Donington, humiliating Prost off the circuit as well as on it, claimed a record sixth win at Monaco and finished the season with victories in Japan and Australia, the last of his life. For much of the season, however, he was impotent against the might of the Williams, a Williams which duly delivered Prost the title. A sense of injustice – which many considered the height of hypocrisy – festered inside Senna and affected his driving, particularly through the middle part of the year.

More were subscribing to the belief that the mantle of Formula One's fastest driver may pass to Schumacher. His season had been tardy in gathering momentum, largely because Benetton had been late producing their new car, complete with in-vogue driver aids, advanced technological weapons such as active suspension and traction control. Semi-automatic gearboxes were regarded as standard. He had third place and fastest lap in Brazil, second at Imola, third and fastest lap in Spain, second and fastest lap in Montreal, third and fastest lap in France, second at Silverstone. He was carried to his home Grand Prix, at Hockenheim, on a wave of nationalism and glowing tributes from his peers.

Overleaf Irresistible, raw speed.

Brundle, who had moved on to Ligier, said: 'Right now he's driving better than anyone in Formula One. Senna looks as if he's backing off a bit, but Schumacher is doing the business. He's brilliant.' He later added: 'I felt for some time he was the fastest out there and, even before Senna died, I had been convinced that in terms of raw speed he was.'

Patrese, enduring an exasperating 1993 season in the other Benetton, was gracious enough to say: 'Any driver who comes into Formula One and after his first full season has a win and finishes third in the Championship has to be good. He was ahead of Senna and Berger and they both had better cars. This year he has the confidence, he knows he is very strong and has 120 per cent motivation. He is in his explosive moment. From the speed point of

Senna at his brilliant best – Donington, 1993.

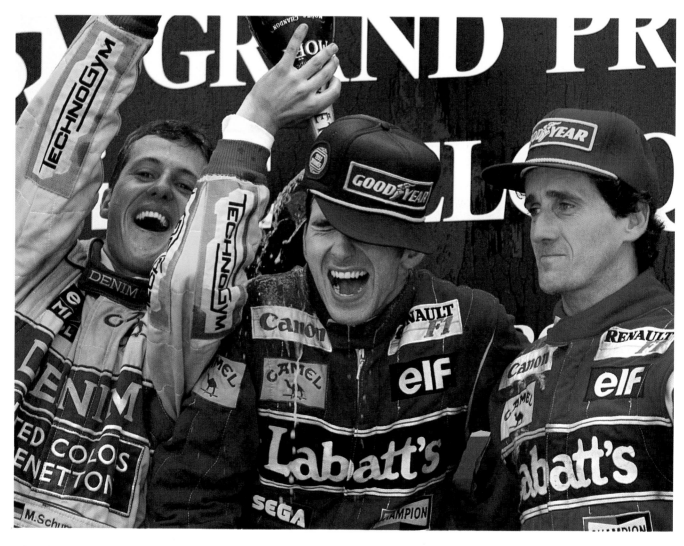

view he is already maybe the quickest with Senna. It is not so much his speed as his maturity which has surprised me. Perhaps, though, he will have to improve on the politics. It seems that if you want to be world champion you must play politics and be a little on the bad side, otherwise you find this world is very tough. But I don't see any young ones at the moment who can match his pace.'

Certainly the 39-year-old Patrese could not and the pressure took its toll. While Schumacher calmly and methodically went about his work, the Italian thrashed around the technical permutations in desperate, and futile, search of solutions. Or miracles. The team admitted they had been too hasty in unloading Brundle, and Patrese, tired and demoralised, would leave Formula One at the end of the season with a record 256 appearances to his credit.

Schumacher could not obstruct Prost's path towards the title that day at Hockenheim, but second place in front of his countrymen was gratifying enough. 'Last year I was third, this year second, so maybe next year I will be first,' he said.

Podium party with Hill and Prost at Spa, 1993.

Another second place at Spa, ever evocative Spa, sustained the flow of points yet Schumacher was only too aware his second year in Formula One had failed to yield a win. By race day at Estoril, Portugal, he was showing the first signs of dismay. 'The car is unpredictable. I went to sleep with data in my eyes,' he said. The team lamented a catalogue of misfortune. The upward curve was in danger of plunging back to earth.

And then, against the odds and their own expectations, Schumacher and Benetton won, ahead of Prost, who was happy enough to secure his fourth World Championship. 'When I think of all the problems we have had and how hard the team has worked, it is fantastic that it ends like this,' Michael said.

In effect it did end like that. Retirements in Japan and Australia left Schumacher on 52 points, fourth in the Championship. Senna was runner-up, Damon Hill third. That pair would represent Williams in 1994 following Prost's decision to quit. Senna had his wish at last. So had Frank Williams. Surely their partnership would be irresistible.

If Benetton were to compete they had to be better prepared. The car, to be powered by the new Zetec-R Ford engine, would have to be built and

Together at last – Ayrton Senna and Frank Williams.

tested ahead of the first race. Before all that, however, they had the more pressing business of renegotiating the services of their much coveted No. 1 driver. Ron Dennis, managing director of McLaren, who were using Peugeot engines for 1994, overtly approached Schumacher in the hope of filling the void left by Senna. In the event Schumacher stayed at Benetton with an improved deal.

Schumacher looked forward to the new season with regulation optimism, and a little more besides. Surgery had cleared up niggling knee problems and winter testing had generally gone to plan. He anticipated challenging more consistently for wins and achieving more wins, but the Championship? No, he was with the rest. It had to be Senna.

A setback to Benetton's preparations was an accident in testing which left Schumacher's latest team-mate, J J Lehto, badly injured. The Finn would miss the start of the Championship and be replaced by the young Dutchman, Jos Verstappen. As Lehto recovered, Schumacher and Senna

Opposite Jos Verstappen, team-mate in 1994.

Schumacher puts Senna under pressure in Brazil, 1994.

were attempting to heal their public rift. Both insisted they had no personal problems. Now all they wanted was to race. Gentlemen, start your engines.

Senna, predictably, took pole in Sao Paulo, immediately ahead of Schumacher, but few could have predicted what was to follow. Schumacher recovered from a sloppy start to regain second place from Jean Alesi, in a Ferrari, and pursued the Williams. He followed Senna into the pits for their first scheduled stops and, thanks to the slick work of his crew – a crucial factor in this race and those that lay ahead – re-emerged with the lead. Schumacher pushed on and 'never felt under pressure'. If he did have any lingering anxieties they disappeared 15 laps from the end, when Senna, striving too hard, slid off.

Brundle, who had filled that vacancy at McLaren, said of Schumacher: 'The guy is awesome. He and Senna were in a class of their own, but he got Senna rattled. Schumacher did his job without mistakes and did it brilliantly.'

The second race, at a new Formula One venue, Aida, in Japan, and run as

Opposite Senna takes his place –
pole – on a starting grid for the
last time at the 1994 San
Marino Grand Prix.

the Pacific Grand Prix, doubled Schumacher's lead over the favourite. Again Senna beat Schumacher to pole, but again Senna went off, this time punted by Mika Hakkinen's McLaren at the first corner. Schumacher cruised to victory. As he and Benetton savoured their prosperity, Senna and Williams stepped up their work-rate to remedy a car the Brazilian found difficult to drive. He could not contain his disbelief that the Benetton, by contrast, looked so driveable. He could not accept it was all down to Schumacher. Driver aids had been banned for this year, but had all the aids, traction control for instance, been removed?

The suspicion, flown by Senna, hovered in the air over the Autodromo Enzo e Dino Ferrari and the San Marino Grand Prix. The great man was said to be broody. Others who saw him that weekend reported he seemed no more or less intense than usual. He was, however, shaken by Rubens Barrichello's accident on the Friday. His young compatriot escaped serious injury, as drivers usually did, and few thought any more of it.

On the Saturday the younger members of the Formula One fraternity – and there were many, including Schumacher – encountered something entirely new and horrifying: death on the track. Roland Ratzenberger, a relative unknown from Austria, driving for Simtek, a relatively unknown team from Britain, crashed into a wall at almost 200 mph and was killed. It was the first Formula One fatality for eight years, the first at a Grand Prix for 12 years.

There would be no time for the sport to recover from the shock. Twenty-four hours later Senna, the most famous driver in the world, competing for Williams, the leading team in the world, started from pole, as ever, followed by Schumacher, as ever, and on the seventh lap went straight on at Tamburello, a flat-out, sweeping left-hander, and plunged into the wall. The 34-year-old Brazilian was pronounced dead that evening in hospital.

One year on, and the drivers
remember Ayrton at Imola.

Since then there has been time – time to acknowledge Senna was dreadfully unlucky and that the fates conspired wickedly against the sport and all who love it that weekend in Italy. Equally, it had to be recognised Formula One had enjoyed years of unbroken good fortune and, although some of the measures ordered to improve safety standards in the wake of the tragedies were driven by panic, a critical self-analysis was overdue.

Senna's death in particular, of course, stunned a global audience and many found the decision to continue with the race repulsive. Hakkinen, who finished third, was roundly condemned for celebrating on the rostrum. Schumacher, who won, was conspicuously restrained. All the drivers said they were unaware of the severity of the crash, but Schumacher patently sensed revelry would be inappropriate.

Looking back, he now says: 'Accidents are part of Formula One and I have seen many accidents that looked worse than Ayrton's. There was Zanardi's at Spa, which looked really awful. That looked worse than Ayrton's but he jumped out. He was bruised, but he was okay. Then you see an accident like Ayrton's which, sure, was heavy, but... At the time I thought, "He's out of the race and maybe he won't be able to race at the next Grand Prix", but that was the worst I could imagine from that accident. He was very unlucky.

'The point is that I wasn't able to see or know what was going on at that stage. I didn't know what his condition was. An accident happens, you stay on the grid, you don't know anything. You don't see any pictures, you don't get any information. What you do know from experience is that a driver in these circumstances is taken to hospital and you have to go on.'

A sense of guilt hung over the entire paddock after the race, and Michael felt its weight more than most. He returned to the sanctuary of the team motorhome and wept. Di Spires, 'Mum' to the Benetton crew, recalls: 'He cried his eyes out. He said it was his fault because he pushed Ayrton too hard, which it wasn't of course. But he was heartbroken and we tried to comfort him. We were all so upset, though. It was awful.'

The fragile human being had taken over from the hard professional and in the days that followed he had to convince himself, in a test at Silverstone, he could go on to the next race. He came through the test and turned up for the next race, on his doorstep at Monaco.

Senna, too, had a place in the Principality. He had also made the race his own in recent years, his total of six wins eclipsing Graham Hill's record. No more poignant setting, therefore, for Schumacher's accession to the throne of Formula One. He was Senna's natural successor, but for a 25-year-old it was a formidable responsibility. Off the track he accepted it by becoming a leader of the revamped Grand Prix Drivers' Association and an activist for safer cars and circuits. On the track he accepted it by proving he was now the best driver in Grand Prix racing.

He began at Monaco by taking pole, recording the fastest lap and winning

Negotiating Barcelona's slow chicane stuck in fifth gear, 1994.

the race. In Spain he had pole, fastest lap, but second place to Hill. Was he disappointed? 'Not at all,' he responded, explaining that he had driven more than half the race stuck in fifth gear. Try to imagine that in relation to your own road car. No, you cannot. Nor could many of Schumacher's opponents. Patrick Head, the technical driving force at Williams, said: 'If that is true, we might as well all pack in.' Schumacher described, in a disarmingly matter of fact way, how he had applied his economical sportscar technique to the task. There are those who believe it was his greatest performance.

In Canada normal service was resumed: pole, fastest lap, win. In France he was upstaged in qualifying by the Williams of Hill and the Williams of Nigel Mansell, taking a highly lucrative busman's holiday from IndyCars to spice up the Grand Prix show. Undoubtedly he rattled Hill's cage. In the race, however, Schumacher speared his car between the two Williams and went on to collect another 10 points. He had six wins and a second from seven races. The crown awaited just around the corner. Or so everyone assumed.

At Silverstone Schumacher, and the Championship, encountered a new twist. Second on the grid, he accelerated past the pole man, Hill, at the start of the parade lap. According to the rules, drivers must hold station. Anyone who does not is liable to be relegated to the back of the grid. The start of the race had to be aborted so they began the procedure again, and again the Benetton shot ahead of the Williams.

If Schumacher hoped to gain an actual or psychological advantage at the start he was to be disappointed. Hill, on home ground, pulled clear as the stewards considered what action to take against Schumacher. They decided to impose a five-second penalty and informed his team. There was not, Benetton maintained, any mention of 'stop-and-go' so their driver was not called in. When Schumacher was shown the black flag no-one should have been in doubt. But still his team declined to take that step and became embroiled in anxious negotiations with officials. Eventually Schumacher came in for his stop-and-go penalty and effectively conceded the race to Hill, but that was not the end of the matter.

Nor was it when the stewards reprimanded Benetton and fined driver and team $25,000. FIA's World Sports Council, after launching an inquiry, stripped Schumacher of his six points from Silverstone and gave him a two-race ban. If he appealed he would be free for the next race, the German Grand Prix, but risk a heavier sanction. On the face of it a wretched dilemma, and yet how could he let down his own people waiting to see him at Hockenheim? He could not.

Benetton were also further punished, fined $500,000 for disobeying the stewards' orders in Britain, plus $100,000 for delaying the handing over of 'source codes' for their electronic systems, which FIA had instructed them to produce several weeks earlier. Here, many suspected, was revealed the undercurrent of this entire acrimonious affair. Doubts about the legality of the Benetton had coursed through the sport and a denouncement of President Max Mosley's stewardship of FIA by the team's managing director, Flavio Briatore, can scarcely have courted sympathy in the corridors of power.

Mosley, of course, rejected any notion of a personal vendetta and Briatore, of course, was adamant his cars were legal. The upshot for Formula One was

Schumacher is black-flagged at the 1994 British Grand Prix.

The fireball horror of Hockenheim, 1994.

that it might have a Championship contest again. Should the ban be upheld, Hill would be in with a chance.

Incensed though defiant, Schumacher and Benetton arrived at Hockenheim determined to contain the tide rising against them, but again their walls were breached. The team had a problem refuelling Verstappen's car, petrol sprayed and ignited. For a few frightening seconds the Benetton was engulfed in flames before the crew managed to put out the fire. Mercifully the young driver scampered away with only minor burns and the mechanics also escaped serious injury.

The team's reputation, however, was to be further damaged by an official accusation they tampered with the refuelling rig, implying they risked the safety of their personnel and others to save time at the pit stop. Benetton countered by claiming they had removed a filter with the knowledge of FIA's technical delegate. The threat of expulsion from the Championship stalked Benetton for several weeks and before all that was resolved they had anguish enough to occupy them.

Schumacher's engine spluttered to submission at Hockenheim and Hill's second place narrowed the title gap to 27 points. Schumacher's consummate victory in Hungary, with Verstappen third, was as much a statement to the authorities as it was retaliation in the Championship fight. When Schumacher crossed the line at Spa ahead of Hill it seemed he was comfortably in command again, even if he should have to serve that two-race ban.

Darkness had descended on the Ardennes and Hill had long since departed when it was announced the Englishman was the winner of the race because Schumacher had been disqualified. The 10 mm skidblock beneath the Benetton – fitted to all cars to reduce cornering speeds – had been measured at less than the 9 mm allowed at the end of the race. The team argued the unusually high rate of wear was caused when the car went over a kerb, but the stewards were unimpressed. Two days later Schumacher's appeal against the two-race ban was rejected. If Hill won those two Grands Prix, in Italy and Portugal, the title protagonists would go into the final three races separated by just one point.

A few days before FIA also turned down the Spa appeal, Schumacher was reported to have said he might seek a new team if he became convinced Benetton had been 'doing things behind my back which were forbidden'. Benetton continued to protest their innocence and Schumacher looked on from afar, helpless as Hill duly closed the gap.

During the week leading to the Grand Prix of Europe, at Jerez, Schumacher and Hill tested at Estoril. Schumacher took the opportunity to deliver a cold and calculated castigation of his rival. He dismissed Hill as a 'second rater' and said winning the Championship now would be all the more satisfying because his season had been reduced from 16 to 12 races. He contended, however, that he would not have had a hope of the title if Senna had been alive.

They posed for a phoney picture of truce at the Spanish circuit before Schumacher and his crew outwitted Hill and his men with their race strategy. The gap was now five points. But in torrential rain at Suzuka, Hill, giving

Phoney truce with Hill at Jerez, 1994.

Hill gets the better of his rival
this time, Suzuka, 1994.

perhaps his finest performance, and Williams turned the tables. One race to go in Adelaide, and one point separating them. It had come down to a winner-takes-all decider.

What happened on the 36th lap of the 1994 Australian Grand Prix is now lodged in sporting folklore. Collisions and controversies were nothing new and this pair would be involved in more during 1995. But this collision and controversy ended the World Championship – in Schumacher's favour. The German, hounded by the Englishman, lost control into a corner and smacked a wall. The Benetton came back across the track as Hill loomed. Schumacher's instincts told him to defend his position, Hill's to take his opportunity and attack. Hill was not aware the Benetton was badly damaged and that he could afford to bide his time. He went for it and they crashed, the Benetton flipping into the air and out of the race. Hill limped back to the pits but also out of the race. Schumacher, standing behind the mesh fencing at the side of the track, was told he was world champion.

Schumacher deflected any suggestions of foul play and Hill took the outcome with dignity, only confiding later that his opponent 'was history and

he knew it'. The general view, shared by Mosley and Ecclestone, was that Formula One had the right drivers' champion in Schumacher and the right constructors' champion in Williams. They had also had a gripping and contentious finale. The world was talking about Grand Prix motor racing, so why should they complain?

Looked at another way, it had been an unsatisfactory conclusion to a hugely unsatisfactory season. Schumacher takes the point but gives these reflections two years on.

'I believe it is clear we deserved the Championship because we were much better prepared, in terms of strategy, than anyone else. We had a very good car until FIA decided to change the rules, which hit us most, and I had four races taken away, and yet we still won. I still trust the team 100 per cent when they say there was no cheating. I know it's not easy to accept a team not so long in the business and as young as we were can come in and beat everybody the way we did, and that's the point which brought up the criticism at the time. But I think we proved, under very hard examination, that there was nothing wrong and we beat the other teams as we had done before, and you can't do better than that.

'In life you have ups and downs and that was the situation I had at Benetton, but I never had thoughts about actually quitting because of that. You occasionally have moments when you wonder why things have to be like

The fateful collision at Adelaide…

70

...and Michael is hailed champion by his team.

this, and think, "Why are you doing this to us?" But then I realise I still love what I'm doing, so I go on and I don't regret the course I have taken.'

That includes the course he took in the fateful split second at Adelaide. He is content to stand back and let others point the finger at Hill for being too impatient.

'You don't deviate when you don't have to deviate,' Schumacher says. 'It is quite clear to many experienced drivers that they would have reacted differently. They would have waited a bit and passed me when they knew it was right and safe to do so. I don't think it's necessary to go more deeply into that. Of course it was not the way I wanted it to end but we won the Championship over the season, not one race.

'We had many highlights to look back on with satisfaction. The race at

Barcelona, where I had only fifth gear, was certainly one. So was Jerez, my first race back after the ban and we won with a great team effort. Also in Hungary, after all the stories about what happened at Hockenheim and a lot of people considered we were cheating with the refuelling and so on, but we beat everybody in the way we had before.'

In the hour of his triumph at Adelaide Schumacher, Germany's first world champion, paid a moving tribute to the late Ayrton Senna, the man he felt should and would have taken the title that 1994 season. 'I have said it many times and I still say it, I would not have beaten Ayrton for that Championship,' he now reiterates.

Much as he was convinced he deserved it ahead of Hill, he knew that in the eyes of the world he wore a tainted crown. That merely strengthened his resolve to retain it, emphatically and beyond all dispute, in 1995. He would accomplish his mission with an imperious manner that smacked of vengeance. He would have his now ritual tangles with Hill, but even then he generally emerged commanding the moral high ground.

Britain's Johnny Herbert, who had made his Formula One debut with Benetton in 1989, returned to the team late in 1994 and was given the job alongside Schumacher for 1995. Herbert, like Brundle, pledged to compete with his team-mate. Unlike Brundle, he declined to adjust his sights and would complain to the end that he was not given a fair chance.

Schumacher was undeniably lavished with most of the attention and Benetton's managing director, Flavio Briatore, made no attempt to disguise his policy. He was charged with delivering results and he figured that by focusing the team's effort and resources on Schumacher he was going the best way about achieving his objective. His No. 1 driver did not let him down.

The Benetton now had the Renault power Williams had enjoyed and Schumacher clocked the fastest lap en route to victory at the opening race in Brazil. It was not, however, quite as simple as that and the new season came in as the old had gone out, in controversy. Schumacher was disqualified after fuel samples taken from Benetton and Williams were found not to comply with samples approved by FIA. At a subsequent hearing it was decided the teams alone should be punished, so Schumacher and Hill's partner, David Coulthard, who finished second, were reinstated.

Schumacher was also involved in an embarrassing mystery over his weight. On the Thursday before the race he was weighed at 77 kilos, after the race at 71.5 kilos. His explanation was that he had eaten rather too well earlier in the week and then proffered flimsy reasoning about water consumption and the timing of his visits to the toilet. The laughs were a touch feeble, too, and did not amuse those still sceptical about events the previous season. Any sort of weight saving is useful in the overall car/driver combination and this whiff of subterfuge was something he could have done without.

Schumacher was well beaten into third place by Hill and Jean Alesi for

Hill savours the opportunity to overtake the champion in the 1995 Argentine Grand Prix.

Ferrari in Argentina and, after stopping for slicks on a drying track at Imola, spun off. One year on from the deaths of Ratzenberger and Senna, he had not relished this weekend and was thankful to leave unscathed.

His Championship campaign was still stuck in the low gears, but Spain changed all that. he took pole and dominated the race. At Monaco Hill pipped him for pole and led the early part of the race. But Schumacher altered his strategy, opting for one pit stop rather than two, and again outsmarted the British driver. A gearshift problem interrupted Schumacher's progress in Canada yet a late and exhilarating charge to fifth place and two points assumed greater significance in light of Hill's retirement. Both were back on the podium in France, but Schumacher had the top step.

They travelled north to Silverstone with Schumacher 11 points clear and looking set for another title. But remember what happened in 1994. Schumacher certainly did. Hill stoked up the contest by describing his arch adversary as a 'clone'. Somewhere in Germany that was misunderstood as 'clown' and translated accordingly. In the race Hill closed on Schumacher and appeared to have him on the ropes. He thrust the Williams inside the Benetton. Schumacher stuck to his line, they collided and were out of the

The championship protagonists
spin off in formation at
Silverstone in 1995.

race. An enraged Schumacher blamed Hill and most observers did likewise, although both were officially reprimanded. Perhaps the most pertinent judgement was delivered by Hill's boss, Frank Williams, who apologised to Benetton on behalf of his driver and reportedly called him 'a prat'. The race was won by Herbert, his first in Formula One.

Hill had pole in Germany and promptly threw everything away, leaving Schumacher to win at last in front of his countrymen. Hockenheim was whipped into a frenzy of patriotism much as Silverstone had been at the height of Mansell's career. Schumacher was delirious. Fortunes, and moods, changed in Hungary. Hill had 10 points, Schumacher none. Next stop Spa, a recurring landmark in Schumacher's career, and this year it signified one of the great drives.

Typically shifting conditions caught out the champion in qualifying and he was stranded in 16th position on the grid, while Hill was eighth. By the 15th lap of the race, however, they were second and first respectively, Hill forfeiting the advantage to take on wet tyres in an intensifying shower. Schumacher stayed out on slicks, à la Senna, and resisted Hill's challenges for a couple of spellbinding, wheel-banging laps. It was a critical period because although Hill eventually went through, the rain ceased and he had to pit for slicks.

Hill peels off for his 10-second penalty as Schumacher heads for victory at Spa, 1995.

The appearance of the safety car after another, heavier downpour, revived Hill's hopes but a stop-and-go penalty and a spin sealed his fate. Hill and his team protested about Schumacher's 'weaving and blocking' tactics and the stewards concluded Williams had a case. They gave Schumacher a one-race ban, suspended for four races. He was furious and many neutrals sympathised with him. Hadn't he just put the racing back into Formula One? At least he still had his 10 points and, after the verdict of 1994, they were all the sweeter.

Monza was almost a re-run of Silverstone. Hill pushed Schumacher from the back, although his vision had been obscured by Taki Inoue's Arrows. They spun into the gravel and marshals had to restrain Schumacher as he climbed out of his car and turned towards Hill. They made their regular visit to the stewards and this time Hill left with a suspended one-race ban. Again in a re-run of Silverstone, Herbert picked up the pieces and won.

Coulthard claimed his maiden Formula One victory in Portugal as Schumacher tightened his hold on the Championship. He surprised Hill with an audacious overtaking manoeuvre at a tight bend to plunder an important second place. Better was to come for the German at this second home race of the season, the Grand Prix of Europe at the Nurburgring. The new 'Ring is a pale imitation of the old, but Schumacher's performance was worthy of the

The vanquished Hill graciously acknowledges Schumacher's 'best win', at the Nurburgring, 1995.

greatest arena. He fended off Hill with characteristic aggression and was equally uncompromising in overtaking the long-time leader, Alesi.

Hill, who crashed out 10 laps from the end, applauded Schumacher and gave him a thumbs up sign from the side of the track as the Benetton went by on its slowing down lap. Back in the paddock the Williams driver virtually conceded the title to Schumacher, who led by 27 points with three races remaining. 'I've no complaints this time. Hats off to the guy, he's a bloody good racing driver.'

Schumacher became the youngest double champion with a comprehensive win in the Pacific Grand Prix and completed Benetton's first Constructors' Championship success with victory in Japan. It was his ninth of the season, equalling Mansell's record of 1992. Alas for Schumacher, he could not go one better. He and Alesi grappled for a narrowing piece of tarmac and suffered the consequences. Hill's easy win was some consolation but the final Championship tally told the story of 1995: 102–69 to Schumacher.

'It was good to win the Championship the way I won it because there was still a lot of talk about '94 and some people could still not accept we had won fairly that year,' he says. 'What we did in '95 was probably the best way to convince them. Even though we had the Renault engine many of the races were tough. The Williams car had developed and the competition was very hard.

'But that made it all the more enjoyable. Winning the races the way I did was the most satisfying part. With respect to Nigel, it was very obvious the Williams package he had in '92 was by far the best and nobody could get close to them. He lapped almost every car. It was not so obvious we were going to win. We had to fight to win and Hill said he had the best car. We made it because we did a better job than anyone else.

'To equal the record number of wins was a credit to all the team and the wins themselves were very special. I thought for some time that Spa was the best and certainly it will always give me particular satisfaction, but having watched the video of Nurburgring a number of times to study situations and the other drivers, I have to say that is my best. Not just because it was in Germany but because I had to be at my best and we had to get everything right.

The double champion shares his moment of triumph with his crew, Aida, 1995.

'Because the Williams was so good and Damon was often running with me we had some incidents which made me angry at the time. At Monza and Silverstone, in particular, he just lost control of himself. It was as if it was too much for him. But I don't see any purpose in going on about that now. These were racing situations, they happen. The result at the end was right. Again. Some people, I think Bernie included, said Damon had lost the Championship again, but I do not believe that is correct. Benetton and I won the Championship.

'Other drivers had a problem with the Benetton because it was very critical, never a solid car. For me it was not a problem, I was able to handle it. I made the most of it and was always prepared to do that. This was the attitude of the team. We worked together, all going in the same direction. That relationship was the important thing. The blend, the understanding, the togetherness made everything so much easier. We overlooked nothing. Everybody believed – I will not say we were convinced because that sounds arrogant – but we just believed in ourselves and what we were doing. We always tried our best and never gave up at any time.

'From the early days we developed a very good way of working together.

Luciano Benetton (left) and Flavio Briatore (top) lead the 'family' celebrations after Michael's second Championship success.

Hey, Watch my car! Schumacher and Alesi have their coming together at Adelaide, 1995, before changing places in 1996.

Everybody had clear territories to work in. Flavio Briatore was the managing director, mainly concentrating on the financial aspects. He gave others the freedom to do their jobs. Ross Brawn ran the team, the technical side, and gave people a lot of opportunities to develop their own creativity and so get the best out of themselves. My engineer was Pat Symonds and I would say he was the best working in this area. I had a close personal relationship with Pat as well as a good working relationship with him. Also with Ross, and they developed into a good combination.

'At the beginning there was a bit of tension between people in these important positions, but in the end they came to appreciate each other, respect each other and see the advantage of working together. We built on the relationship, especially from the end of 1993 onwards. There was no unpleasantness, no in-fighting, no jealousy. It is a situation you do not find often but we had it and it made us what we were, champions.'

And that is where he left them. He departed to forge new relationships and meet perhaps the ultimate challenge.

What It Takes

Those who excel in any activity are probed, interrogated and examined for the secret of their success and to some extent it is a futile exercise. Those touched by genius are very few and usually beyond analysis anyway. What can we make of a mere boy who created music the way Mozart did? But for the most part the outstanding musicians, artists and sportsmen and women are simply mortals blessed with talent they have been prepared to nurture and even exploit. The great performers have always been those willing to dirty their skills and lather their gifts in sweat. Michael Schumacher is the latest, classic example in motor racing.

Ask him to explain his inherent talent and he is disarmingly yet unpretentiously brief: 'It came to me because I just loved driving.' And so it is with footballers, cricketers, golfers and tennis players. The sheer joy of the sport draws them into its embrace. How close and how long the love affair endures depends on opportunity and motivation. Professionalism takes the sports person into a different sphere. Ability alone is not enough. Now comes the test of that dedication, commitment and, at the pinnacle, the selfish streak that may lose friends but win championships.

As we shall hear later, Schumacher recognised in Ayrton Senna and Alain Prost not only natural sublimity but also uncompromising determination to develop and improve what they possessed in order to become the best in Formula One. Schumacher's career has been a similarly concerted, calculated campaign to harness the ability that became evident in the boy who 'just loved driving'.

As we have already heard, he was fortunate enough to have the opportunity to race. His father, his various sponsors and then Mercedes provided the resources and facilities to develop and improve those fundamental driving skills. But then motor racing history is littered with the broken dreams of rich kids who had the resources and facilities, yet never the genuine talent, or commitment, to make the grade. Schumacher is unlikely ever to be accused of profligacy. Some say his single-minded pursuit of excellence is obsessive, almost repulsive. Some said the same of Senna. It depends what you want. Senna and Schumacher left no-one in doubt what they wanted on their way to the summit.

Opposite The artist at work.

Overleaf Michael masters the opposition and the elements to claim his first win for Ferrari, Barcelona, 1996.

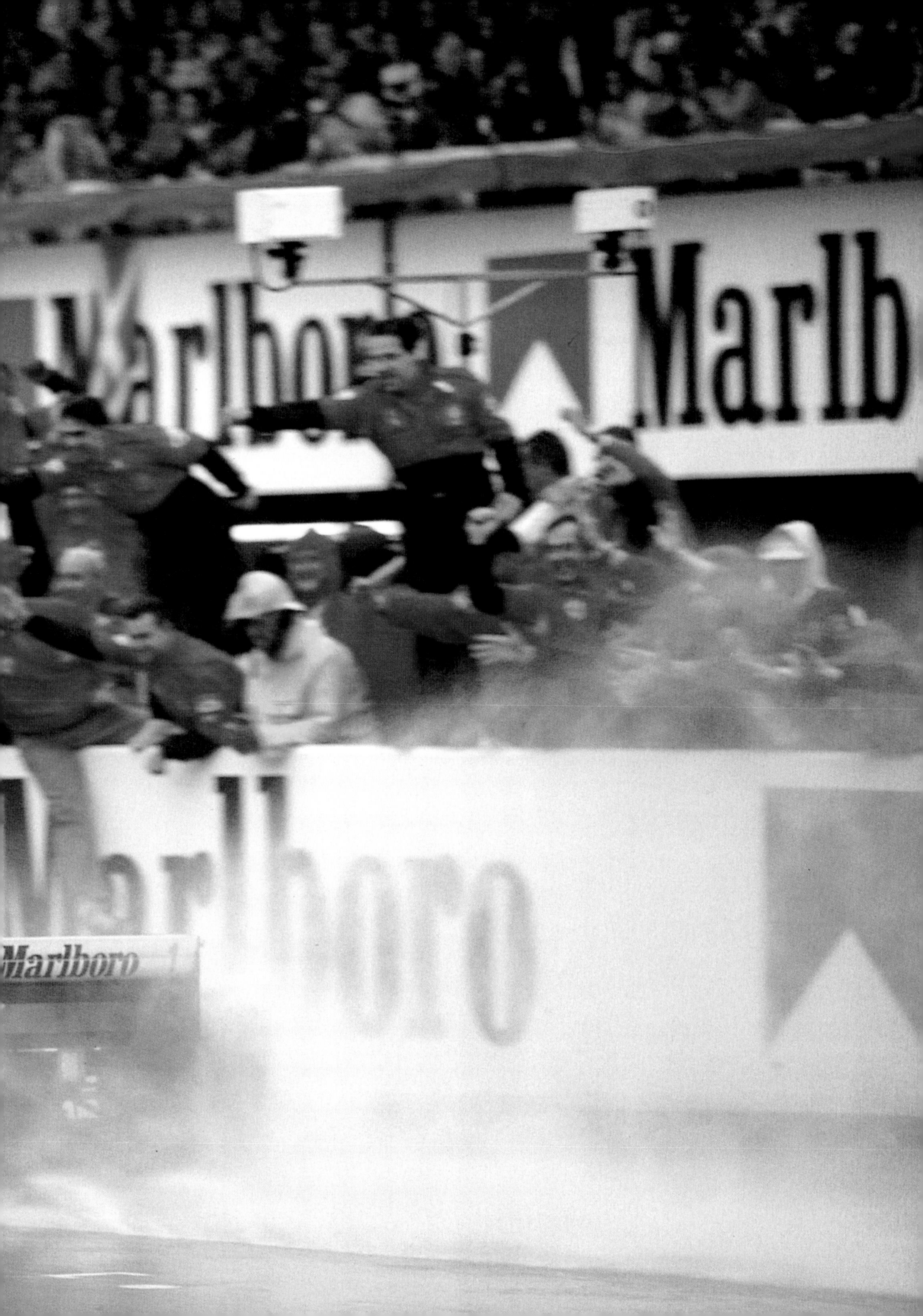

Marlboro
Marlb
Marlboro
Marlboro

The best drivers have what motor racing experts refer to as 'feel' for the car. Schumacher puts it like this: 'You have to have the senses in your whole body, that come up to your brain, and then, in the end, you have to transfer the information to the steering wheel. It is how you do this that is the difference between drivers, between those who are sensitive, who have more feeling, and those who may be as sensitive but are not able to translate that into their driving. This is something you either have or you do not.'

The cognoscenti of this business also suggest Schumacher has found an advantage in his driving technique, his use of the throttle as well as the wheel through corners.

He says: 'Most drivers do use the throttle, but the difference is the way you use the throttle. Some are very jerky, some are very smooth. My style is to be smooth and consistent, or at least try to be. I try to be always on the limit, not just in a part of the corner but all the way through it. This, I believe, is the major difference between drivers. Some are on the limit coming out of the corner but most of the time they are not on the limit going in, or

Schumacher shows Williams the way round Jerez, 1994.

mid-corner. They are losing out in this region. They are using the throttle coming out of the corner but that cannot make up for what is already lost.

'Over the course of a lap and a full race distance, that can obviously make a big difference, perhaps the difference between making pole position and not making pole, or winning the race and finishing second or third.'

Schumacher was initially carried along not only by the feel but also an unstoppable momentum. Out of the pleasure, that early, innocent 'fun', came the realisation that he could pilot a racing car faster than most, and that, in turn, propelled him to another level. The momentum was now self-generating.

'I think the greatest sensation you can get from anything you do in life is the satisfaction you get when you feel you can do it really well, that you can be very good at it, better than others. That, for me, is the main satisfaction in driving the car, feeling I am driving the car on the limit and at the end getting the lap time I have worked for through the lap, or the result I have worked for through the whole race.

'That is where I get the satisfaction. I get a feeling in the car whether I am going quickly or slowly. The important thing is to try and achieve the maximum. If you know you have then you say to yourself, "I can be satisfied". You know if you are doing it right and you know if you are doing it, in my case, better than the rest of the world. That is the biggest satisfaction.

'When they landed on the moon they could not explain it in the way that perhaps the world was hoping and expecting them to say. It is a little like that with Formula One. All the followers and fanatical supporters of Formula One have their excited view of it, so you cannot look at it as people do from the outside. It is like when you dream of a fantastic car and then, when you drive it, you get used to it. And then it's not such a great mystery and wonder to you any more.'

Schumacher's cool analysis of his 'normal' working environment belies the pressures of the job and it is reassuring to hear he is not immune to those forces. Unsurprisingly, he has a strategy to minimise the effects.

'There is stress on the circuit and it is there for all of us,' he says. 'So when I get out of the car I try to relax as much as possible. I do not try to force things or people. What I do look for, however, is order. There has to be good organisation and method to work effectively. If you have chaos you have an unpredictable situation, and to drive in Formula One when things are unpredictable is the most dangerous situation you can have. The whole thing has to be safe. That is the priority. You must approach it all from the safety point of view. The best way you can ensure this is by being relaxed.'

Schumacher maintains he has been faithful to this philosophy of order and relaxation throughout his Formula One career. At Benetton, essentially a British team, he found kindred spirits. Organisation was second nature and together they developed a methodical working practice that surpassed all others. This had also long been a haven of 'cool dudes', so they knew how to unload and unwind.

On the face of it, Ferrari presented an entirely different proposition and challenge. Despite their almost boundless resources, they were not renowned for discipline and co-ordination. For Gerhard Berger, the move from Ferrari to Benetton in 1996 was a shock to the system. 'At Benetton they work unbelievably hard,' he says. 'If the circuit opens at nine o'clock they push you out of the truck at five to nine to get into the car. When it is five to nine at Ferrari you pick up another espresso.' Schumacher presented himself as the catalyst to change all that. He drew them into his routine, endeavouring to complement traditional flair with essential method and sheer hard work. And then, when a break during testing permitted it, he would join the mechanics in a game of football. They are used to superstars at Maranello, but not superstars who so readily and easily mix with the troops and show a genuine interest in their work and problems.

The concept of a relaxed Schumacher amuses his team-mate at Ferrari,

One of the lads, playing football in a break from testing.

Eddie Irvine. The Ulsterman has had scant testing opportunities because his senior partner has chosen to shoulder the bulk of the responsibility. Asked about his testing, Irvine responded drily: 'I have a man who does that for me.' He later told a press conference that Schumacher 'has a serious relaxation problem. He doesn't know how to do it.'

Schumacher has worked at his profession as few, possibly none, before have. The three-day tests squeezed between fortnightly three-day race meetings around the globe, and technical meetings deep into the evenings make up his regular schedule. Training, sponsorship engagements and media interviews just about consume the rest of his time. Those who deal with him will testify to his 'professionalism', a convenient term to encompass his business-like approach to anything he takes on. He is punctual, polite and respectful with those similarly serious about their work, yet prepared to inject a little humour when he feels it is appropriate.

The romantic notion of motor racing being a pursuit of amateurs and gentlemen disappeared in the early years of the World Championship, which was inaugurated in 1950. A few dedicated playboys and drinkers stood their defiant and unsteady ground through the sixties and even into the seventies, but the conscientious and abstemious were proving ever more irresistible and, come the eighties, the leading drivers were becoming acknowledged as professionals and athletes.

Simply driving a Grand Prix car round a circuit would prove beyond the capabilities of most. In attempting to explain the G-forces experienced by drivers, Nigel Mansell famously suggested a ride in a Formula One car 'would kill your granny'. To manhandle these beasts through corners and along straights of varying characteristics, for an entire race distance – up to 200 miles or two hours in duration – requires considerable strength and stamina. Powerful forearms are essential. So are neck muscles to resist the G-forces.

Despite the greater awareness of the fitness demands, even some of the outstanding drivers were still found physically wanting. Nelson Piquet, three

Eddie Irvine in familiar pose, sitting out testing…

times world champion, collapsed on the podium after a race. Ayrton Senna, also three times world champion, sat motionless in his car for many minutes after a race, the exertions of the ordeal having drained him. Mansell gave more of himself than most in his quest for fulfilment and, after a vain bid to overtake Senna at Monaco in 1992, the year of the Englishman's Championship success, he stumbled, exhausted, at the foot of the royal steps.

To the dismay of all his rivals, Schumacher never looks remotely distressed when he climbs from the cockpit. Damon Hill once remarked, only half jokingly and with understandable envy, that the German 'isn't human'. Such comments make Schumacher smile smugly. If he had a psychological as well as physical advantage, so much the better. 'That is important to me,' he confirms.

From fitness comes the self-assurance, control and total concentration. He expands: 'It applies whenever you get into the car. In testing or practice I don't need any warm-up time before I get into my job. When I am sitting on the grid for the start of a race I am concentrating on the red lights, waiting for them to go out, and that is all you can think about at this stage. During the race I try to stay as calm as possible. Of course there are moments of high tension, but you can imagine what it would be like going round Monaco for

...and an exhausted Mansell, sitting out Senna's victory celebration at Monaco, 1992.

two hours with a heart rate of 170 to 180. You would be exhausted. If you can, as I do, keep it to a maximum of 140 you are obviously going to have an advantage. You do the same job but the other guy is over the limit, while I am not. That is the difference you can get between drivers.

'For sure fitness is one thing, but the other is how you pace yourself in the car. How tough is it for you to run the car on the limit? Some drivers find themselves under so much tension it is not very easy or natural for them to handle it. So it is about fitness, confidence and the ability to make it easy for yourself. Some over-react and have problems, some stay calm and usually benefit because of that.'

As we have heard, Schumacher was obsessed with fitness from an early age. Since arriving in Formula One, he has established new standards of fitness which the rest are having to respond to. Between races and testing he trains for four or five hours a day: cycling, stretching, gym work and some jogging. Before the 1996 season he took on an Indian trainer, Balbir Singh, who guides him through his strict regime.

A balanced and controlled diet is inevitably part of that regime. Schumacher eats little meat and limits his intake of fats. Fibre and carbohydrates figure prominently on his menu. He usually has muesli for breakfast and only light lunches. Pasta is his regular pre-race meal. He also consumes, in common with his peers, seemingly vast quantities of liquid before a race, which is vital but also tends to send drivers scurrying to the toilet at the last minute. That may be nerves, too, of course.

The consumption of alcohol is rigidly contained. 'Of course I enjoy a drink, especially with my friends on special occasions or at parties at the end

The work the fans do not see.

First on two wheels in the other race at Silverstone, 1993.

of the season.' he says. 'On 1st January we had some friends at our home, we drank and had a good time. But from that day drinking was finished. I decided there would be no more alcohol for me until the end of the season. When it was my birthday (3rd January) it was quite difficult because everybody was drinking and saying, "Hey, come on, have a beer". But I had to say "No".'

Schumacher's lead in the field of fitness is now being followed by the likes of Hill, who prepared as never before for the 1996 season, David Coulthard and Jean Alesi, who moved into the vacated seat at Benetton. They all recognised that the ability to sustain pace for anything less than an entire race was no longer good enough.

Martin Brundle says: 'There's no question the guy laid down new guidelines in terms of fitness. He came in with the stamina to maintain his speed from first lap to last. It is one thing to be able to produce a quick lap in qualifying, quite another to pour it on throughout the race. Schuey can and he has given himself a crucial edge because of that.'

The oldest housewives' tales link healthy bodies with healthy minds and modern sportsmen will tell you physical and mental agility are inexorably connected. Schumacher appears to be living, breathing, thinking proof. 'Getting fit is a mental thing as well as physical,' he says. 'It makes me feel good if I know I am fit.' Bernard Dudot, technical director of Renault Sport, worked with Schumacher in 1995 and was astounded by his mental capacity. He recalls: 'Michael would be talking to the team over the radio during the race and be very precise in wanting to know where the other drivers were, wanting to know about their pit stops and so on. He would take in all this

End of the 1994 season, and time to let go.

information and then calmly determine his own strategy. And you had to remind yourself that all the time he was doing this he was also out there on the circuit, racing. He is quite incredible.'

Ross Brawn, technical director of Benetton, is similarly impressed. He says: 'Apart from all the obvious qualities such as pace and competitiveness and motivation, a successful driver, a champion, requires intelligence. The very best are great thinkers, and Michael is no exception. I remember in Portugal in 1995, when he overtook Hill at a point where overtaking wasn't expected, a slow, tight corner. But Michael had thought about it and, to make sure of the grip to pull off the manoeuvre, had taken this unusual line through the corner on a couple of previous laps. He pulled it off. That's the sort of thinking Michael puts into his racing.'

When the hours of testing and de-briefing, the pit stop practice, and attention to the tiniest detail reap reward, Schumacher has his satisfaction. Riccardo Patrese, his team-mate for a season at Benetton, was struck by the young man's diligence and focused sense of purpose. He observed: 'For someone of his age he never does or says anything stupid.'

Schumacher seems mildly surprised Patrese or anyone else should be surprised by that. 'I try to be very particular,' he expands. 'What we are doing here is not a joke. It's a professional thing which, for me, if I want to succeed, has to be done correctly. If I am to fulfil my targets I need to work in a certain way. When I sit in the car and achieve what I planned to achieve, then I have the satisfaction I want.

Taking the lead from Jacques Villeneuve at the 1996 Spanish Grand Prix.

'When I can produce the lap times I wanted, when I go as quickly as I think I can, and when a change to the car gives the result we wanted it to and it does so because I have been very precise, I have the satisfaction I need. I could say to the team "do that" and then go away and have a coffee, a joke, walk around, whatever. That's not my style. It never has been. I work together with the team, professionally.

'That goes back to my days with Mercedes. Even when I was young I worked in a very professional way. I even felt we were not professional enough. I always wanted to go into more detail, to have more information. I did not always have that information and therefore could not make the improvements I wanted, so I really pushed very hard to learn and understand the principles, and to prepare myself for the future.'

His detractors condemn this all-consuming desire for perfection (he has been called an automaton) just as they condemn his ruthlessness on the track. He makes no apologies on either count. Similar accusations were levelled at Senna. Could it be coincidence they are also regarded as two of the pre-eminent drivers in the history of Grand Prix racing? Winning is a serious business, hence Ferrari's willingness to pay Schumacher a reported $25 million a year.

Many question the sanity and morality of motor racing, let alone salaries on that scale. 'People are always asking this and I can understand it,' Schumacher acknowledges. 'What's the point in going round in circles all the time? But then what is the point in 22 people running behind a football? Or

Team-work is vital.

millions of people hitting a tiny ball round a golf course? It's the fascination, the enjoyment. I have found something I just enjoy and can, on top of that, actually do better than others.

'I go back to where I started – go-karts. I still do it because I still feel I can have fun there. It makes me genuinely happy. When I was doing my apprenticeship, changing oil filters in road cars, I didn't have fun doing that. Now I have the possibility to do something I have a lot of fun with, earn a living from and improve myself with other people. I am sure any sportsman will say the same about his sport.

'Of course our sport can be dangerous and we saw how dangerous at Imola in 1994. But in every sport and pursuit in life you can face danger – horse-riding, skiing, whatever. Just going out in a road car can be dangerous. In my view, motor racing is not dangerous as long as you do it within your limits. It becomes dangerous when you go beyond those limits, and that's where a good racing driver, a racing driver who looks after himself, never goes.

'You may have a mechanical problem, but again, this is not unlike other sports. Things can break, things can go wrong. But if they don't it is up to you how much risk you take. It is your choice. I feel I drive within my limits. But even if you go off the circuit in Formula One there is a certain safety level. Think back to Mika Hakkinen's accident at Adelaide in 1995 and imagine going into a wall at 200 kph, as he did, but in a road car. You would be dead. You could not survive that.'

For a while, an agonising, tortuous while, Schumacher feared Hakkinen had not survived that crash. So what does it take for a driver to cope with a situation such as that? Michael admits he had to be persuaded by his boss at Benetton, Flavio Briatore, and Formula One's impresario, Bernie Ecclestone, to get back into his car that day.

'Flavio was afraid I wouldn't get into the car at all,' he ways. 'He took me to Bernie, who showed me the pictures from the in-board camera. This showed me Mika had a mechanical failure and therefore I was able to get in the car again. But if I had seen that a driver as good as Mika could make a mistake and the result was so serious, then I would know I could make a mistake as well and have the same risk as Mika. I wouldn't be comfortable. Until I knew what had happened I felt empty.'

His resolve was examined still more intensely after Senna and Roland Ratzenberger were killed.

'I had to think very seriously about my future and whether I wanted to continue racing. It was the first time I had had to face such a situation in my sport and I did not know if I would be able to go to the next race as confidently as before. Only after a test at Silverstone did I feel I could go on.

Still Michael's great love, as he demonstrates at Magny-Cours, 1996.

'It was very important for me to find out if I did still have this feeling for racing, or whether I could have gone out and thought, "This is all too fast for me... Look, this wall is so close... I can die here... I can die there". If I had

these feelings afterwards – and I certainly had them before the test – I could not have gone on. I remember going round the circuit first of all in a road car and thinking, "How could you have gone so fast here?" Seeing all those walls so close I suddenly appreciated what could happen in Formula One.

'So it was very important for me to sit back in the car and start by going round slowly, then increase the speed to see if I had the natural ability, as before. I told myself not to drive over the limit, be well aware of the dangers around you but still try to be quick. The answer I got within a couple of laps of Silverstone was positive and something I had to find out.

'It is natural that safety has become more important to me than ever before. Yes, I had realised it was important, but what happened at Imola made things different. I started to think more about these things. This is also to do with age. When you get older you think more about many things, you take things easier.

'Yes, there is a risk in Formula One. It's dangerous. But I love this sport and perhaps that is why I try to protect it. I believe in it. The way I live with it is by doing it within my limits. Obviously some drivers are better than others, but what about the bad drivers on the highway?

'In Formula One I believe no-one purposely tries to hit you with the intention of hurting you. If you fight and touch each other you can go off. It has happened in the past and will happen in the future.'

So have the gentlemen drivers gone forever? 'In Formula One, as in so many other activities, the business side has become so strong. You find it even in go-karts now. It has become very serious. To do Formula One correctly and do it well you have to do it seriously.'

To do it correctly each driver will have his own idiosyncrasies, superstitions and rituals. In this regard Schumacher is no different from the rest. Perhaps the last minute dash to the toilet is a case in point. He has another. 'I always get into the car from the same side. You will have to look to see which side.' The evidence of the 1996 season would appear to confirm he always climbs into the cockpit from the left.

Talk of doing it seriously brings us back to Senna and a comparison Michael may not like yet cannot ignore.

'It is wrong, I think, to compare me with Ayrton, but if you want to have success you have to have discipline, and there will always be people who don't like your discipline. If you try to be good to everybody you will probably not have the success. But you have to try to find the right way in between. That's what I always try to do. I don't try to see just the success. I try to achieve the success in a confident way but not by upsetting people. I would rather work together to achieve success than go in my own direction and make people go my way.'

Stepping into the cockpit from his 'lucky' side.

Colleagues and Rivals

The famous duel at the 1991 Spanish Grand Prix. Nigel Mansell *(left)* forces Ayrton Senna into submission.

Any sport at the sharp end is likely to be confrontational, even vindictive. The collision of egoes comes with the narrowing territory. In motor racing the protagonists must negotiate another reality – danger. This intoxicating mix explains much of Formula One's appeal. The stunning cars, the glamour and sheer scale of events are essential elements, of course, but ultimately this is a gladiatorial spectacle, man against man, and therein lies the allure for the masses.

Another factor in the human equation of Grand Prix conflict is the competition between team-mates. The first man a driver has to beat if he wishes to advance is his partner. He is the one other driver operating with the same equipment and resources, and therefore the one driver with whom an accurate comparison is possible. When these two drivers have the best car on the grid and corner the Championship market, the plot thickens. Intrigue and suspicion are rife; overt hostility is almost inevitable.

Down the years the title contest has produced some explosive duels, both between team-mates and drivers of different teams. Four champions of the past decade – Nelson Piquet, Alain Prost, Ayrton Senna and Nigel Mansell – were involved in stirring races against each other but also clashes on and off the track.

To this list of intense rivalries history will add Michael Schumacher v Damon Hill. The routes to the German's two Championship successes with Benetton were littered with the remnants of their skirmishes. They collided on the circuits of Adelaide, Silverstone and Monza, and Hill condemned Schumacher's tactics at Spa-Francorchamps. Verbal blows were exchanged with the ferocity of their racing. Schumacher denounced Hill as 'second rate'. Hill described Schumacher as 'a clone'. A German news agency's miscomprehension of the word and subsequent translation as 'a clown' served to stoke up the feud.

Schumacher views their contretemps as a natural consequence of their rivalry. 'We have been involved in a number of incidents because we want to win races, we want to win Championships, and when you have this situation and all the things around you, these are the things that happen.'

Similarly unamazing is the fact they are not the best of friends out of their cars, although Schumacher contends he has always been willing to foster a relationship with Hill. He argues the Englishman's changes of mood have placed obstacles between them.

'I believe people should be consistent, and this is where I find it difficult to understand Damon,' Schumacher says. 'In our business it is maybe difficult and there are various factors to consider. Damon found himself, in a very short time, in a position to win races and he suddenly became popular. So much happened very quickly, and it was not easy for him.

'In the past I have been scuba diving with Damon, and we've been together in various places, and it is the way he can suddenly change that makes it difficult to understand what is going on inside him. A good example was after the last race of the 1995 season, in Australia. We had a party that night and everybody had a good time. Damon was actually next to me. We had a chat and a drink and it was really good, very easy, the way you feel it should be after the season is finished.

'Next morning, I was at the checkout desk, with my wife, and he comes along, sees us and just runs. He doesn't even say hello, but turns his back on us. Now I cannot understand this. It is bizarre behaviour. But everyone who knows him says this is the way he is. I can't deal with somebody like that. Fortunately, I don't need to. I don't need to be friends with him.'

The perceived need to score psychological points is nothing new to the Schumacher-Hill era and most observers are of the opinion that the former has generally been ahead on this scorecard. A defence put forward for Hill's 'sudden changes' is that he is shy. There are, undeniably, occasions when he looks ill at ease.

He relates an instance of his discomfort with Schumacher: 'It was at the 1995 Grand Prix of Europe, at the Nurburgring. We were both staying at the circuit hotel and one morning I walked out and made for the tunnel to the paddock just as Michael did. It was one of those awkward situations where you don't know whether to walk a little ahead, a little behind, whether to say anything or what. In the end I just said "Cold, isn't it?" Pathetic, really, I know. But it is difficult in our situation.' Hill approached the 1996 season determined not to be drawn into a further crossfire of words, declaring his intention to concentrate on his own affairs. Schumacher was less restrained.

'I can imagine it is very difficult for Damon because he has never been consistently quicker than his team-mate,' Schumacher suggested. 'He has

Opposite For once Schumacher and Damon Hill appear to be in step and in agreement – Magny-Cours, 1993.

Opposite below Another clash of the rivals, this time at Monza, 1995, and Schumacher has to be restrained by marshals as Hill sits in his Williams.

never been a clear No. 1, so he tries to make himself look better than he is. It is normal that he tries to protect himself.

'Damon is one of those who talked a lot about the benefits I had at Benetton, but I would like to put the record straight on this. To say Benetton built a car specially for me is bull. What I had was a car which was made available to me and we made the best out of it. Fortunately, that was enough to achieve the World Championship.

'What I could achieve in a Williams I don't know because I have never been in a Williams,' he smiles, a mite mischievously, 'but I'd say I am quite happy Damon is sitting in a Williams. If there was another driver in this car it might be more difficult for me. Damon is quick, don't misunderstand me, but I am happy to fight against him in a Williams.'

Hill is one of those who has described Schumacher as ruthless. 'Sure,' the German acknowledged. 'I am also twice world champion and Damon has twice been second.'

Schumacher cites, by way of contrast, his relationship with David Coulthard, who partnered Hill at Williams in 1994 and 1995 before joining McLaren Mercedes. 'We were at the same holiday resort in Australia, went horse-riding together, and when we meet each other you sense a certain relationship. I am not saying we are the best of friends, but we understand each other very well. He is a good guy and I like him.

'He is the kind of guy you can have a very hard, fair fight with, then step out of the car and shake hands with. He doesn't complain "that was not fair" or "that was not correct". He is able to accept defeat when he knows he has been beaten. I can cope with guys like this. I don't want to have enemies. I

Mixed company… with Johnny Herbert and David Coulthard at the 1994 Bercy kart meeting in Paris.

don't need them. But obviously Damon has some difficulties with this.'

However, Coulthard has not, as yet, challenged him for the Championship and Schumacher acknowledges the advance of some tyro may one day put him to the sword, just as his emergence tested Ayrton Senna.

'I don't know how I'm going to react when the next young driver comes along and does the same to me,' he admits. 'Time will tell.'

A precocious Schumacher ruffled Senna's feathers on a number of occasions. They clashed at Magny-Cours and again at Hockenheim, during testing, where the Brazilian was led away by McLaren mechanics after grabbing Schumacher by the collar.

Schumacher now says: 'I'm not exactly sad that I had these incidents with Ayrton, but certainly I would be happier if they had not occurred. There were many circumstances where I felt I was not respected at all by him and at certain times he tried to teach me a lesson on the circuit. But from this

Schumacher's Benetton and Senna's McLaren litter the run-off area after their collision in the 1992 French Grand Prix.

A coming together on more amicable terms – Schumacher and Senna at the 1993 British Grand Prix.

base, at the beginning of my Formula One career, I believe I became respected by him and I think I can be proud of that. We got on well at the end.'

Schumacher chose not to join the drivers among the mourners at Senna's funeral, a decision said at the time to have been made because of fears for his safety. Schumacher was, after all, Senna's rival for the Championship and hard on his heels when he plunged into that wall at Imola.

Two years on, Schumacher says: 'Personal safety was one consideration, but it was the smallest. The first point to make is that to feel what I felt at that time it was not necessary to go to church or be present at the funeral. I don't go to church, but I know what I believe, what I think and what my emotions are.

'It would not have been easy to be there because, as I have explained, Ayrton was my idol from way back when I saw him in that go-kart race. But also, at the time, my emotions and feelings about racing were confused. I didn't know if I wanted to continue racing. It was only after that test at Silverstone that I felt I could go on. Without that test I would not have been able to go to the next race feeling sure I could drive normally.

'These were reasons why I did not go to the funeral, but to be honest now, I regret that I wasn't there. It was probably the wrong decision. I have heard it said that some people who went to the funeral were not sincere, but we do not know and I do not judge. Take the situation with Mika. We are not friends. We respect each other, that's it. But even though I don't have a relationship with the guy, when he had his crash at Adelaide I felt he was a part of my life. I wouldn't get back in my car until I found out what had happened. In circumstances like these, it doesn't matter about the relationship. It matters that he is one of you, and you feel it for him.

'I think time, or the lack of it, is one reason why it is just not possible to have real friends in Formula One. I've spoken to Jochen Mass about this and he says that 20 years ago drivers had the time to go on holiday together, sail together and socialise together. Now you race, you test, you go to promotions and there's no time to really enjoy yourself with other drivers. David is a good example here. We had fun in Australia, but there is no time to become real friends. He has a place in Monaco, as I do, but I never know if he is in Monaco, England, Scotland or somewhere else.

'In my early career it was much different. We had lots of fun karting. In Formula Three my team-mate was Frank Schmickler. We went to races together and spent time together between races, enjoying ourselves. It is simply not like that in Formula One.'

It's little surprise Schumacher and Heinz-Harald Frentzen are not the friends they were. Frentzen's former girlfriend, Corinna Betsch, was at Michael's side by the end of 1991 and became Mrs Schumacher in the summer of 1995.

'They had split when Corinna and I came together,' Schumacher insists. 'I have never had a deep conversation with him about this situation because from my point of view there is no reason to ask Heinz-Harald what really happened. They had finished and Corinna and I came together. Now we compete against each other in Formula One it is an interesting story to write about and try to make some fuss over, but it is not the way some people want to present it. If I had taken away his girlfriend while they were still together then I'm sure we would have different, bad things to say against each other. But that is not the case.

'I know it's not very easy for Heinz-Harald. He was the guy left alone and it is always more difficult for the person who has been left. But Corinna and I have been together for a number of years now, we have married, and I have to say I have taken the right decision and Corinna has taken the right decision.

The new champion and his wife-to-be are serenaded at the 1994 FIA awards ceremony.

'Heinz-Harald and I are still okay together. When we see each other we speak. We are not as close friends as we used to be and if we had a situation the other way round I would not wish to be so close to him. I remember after an earlier girlfriend and I split up it was always difficult when I saw her again. There is always someone who feels hurt and I have no reason to wish him unnecessary hurt. There are plenty of people in the world you can meet and be together with.'

Schumacher has sensed copious resentment since his arrival in Formula One, but then he was seen as an upstart threatening to disturb the accepted order of things. He outpaced Andrea de Cesaris and then, more significantly, the triple world champion, Nelson Piquet, at Jordan and Benetton respectively. Piquet left the House of Benetton, to be replaced by Martin Brundle for the 1992 season. Another experienced driver, a sportscar world champion and winner of the Le Mans classic, Brundle declared himself unconcerned about his young partner's rapidly inflating reputation. The Englishman was not renowned for his qualifying, but he was a hugely respected racer and pledged to educate Schumacher in the craft. Four fruitless Grands Prix into the season, he conceded Schumacher was something else and amended his aspirations accordingly.

'Martin was clever after the first three or four races,' Michael recalls. 'He saw the situation and did not make so many promises, and after that his results were very good. He had his best season. It has always been a rather strange relationship between us. Among the Formula One drivers I have to say I have a good and professional relationship with Martin. He is very clever and I respect him very much. He is not just a racing driver, he involves himself in other things, he's an intelligent man. I like him and we have had some good times.

'But I don't think we will become really close friends until one of us finishes racing because there's always a certain unknown within our relationship, a certain uncertainty that you cannot quite work out. I don't know why it is and it's probably a two-way thing. He struggles quite a lot with my jokes. He would try to have a joke with me, give me a little squeeze, but I always knew he had no real answer. I always had the feeling he wanted to have the last tickle, but he never succeeded. He couldn't handle my German humour and when I made an English joke he was lost. We came to understand each other very well. If you go through my team-mates, you can see how close he was to me on the track. Not in qualifying, but in racing he was, how do you say in English? – a pain in the ass.

'I pushed for him to join me at Ferrari. I spoke to the team about this because I knew he was a serious worker, I knew how to work with him and he would have been a good guy to have. For some reason they didn't choose him, but then the choice was theirs.'

Unfortunately for Brundle, his erratic start to the season undermined his long term prospects at Benetton and by the time he had his season back on course it was too late. The Italian, Riccardo Patrese, had already been lined up by his countryman, Flavio Briatore, to join Schumacher in 1993. This, however, was the beginning of the end for Patrese, Formula One's most experienced driver. Shattered by Nigel Mansell at Williams the year before, he was destroyed by his new team-mate at Benetton.

Michael says: 'The good thing about Riccardo was that he never tried to tickle me. That was the difference. There was never any of the tension or competition there was with Martin. Riccardo is always straight, really straight. He certainly tried to find reasons why he was slower than me, but he never tried to be political against me and never tried in any way to slow me down. He always worked for the team. To improve his situation, yes, but always with a thought for the team.

'We had a very, very good year, and that was a year which must have been difficult for him. He was well behind his targets and what he thought he could do, and he was upset. If there were problems, it seemed he was the one who had them. I can understand how difficult it was for him. I'm not sure whether they were always mechanical problems, but I think when you find yourself in a certain situation, going down, and things are not clear to you, then you become less secure. You take it more easily, you reduce your speed, things get on top of you, build up and become worse. Once things are going in this direction they are very hard to stop. That is what happened to Riccardo during that season.

'I remember at Silverstone, when I crashed my car in practice and had to get into his. I went two seconds quicker than he had managed, and I think it showed the truth of the situation. When he was slower than me before it wasn't always the car, it was him. There were certain problems, sure, but sometimes I had them as well and I could live with them. My attitude was

Riccardo Patrese, respected team-mate.

that I knew what I had so either I used it or I didn't. Riccardo's problem was that he could not do that.'

Schumacher had three team-mates in 1994: the Finn, JJ Lehto, the Dutchman, Jos Verstappen, and Britain's Johnny Herbert. Lehto was due to be his partner but a pre-season accident upset that plan and the young test driver, Verstappen, took over. Lehto eventually claimed his place in the team but failed to meet expectations and Verstappen came in again, only to be dislodged late in the year by Herbert. Benetton confirmed Herbert for 1995 and the English driver made even more extravagant forecasts of personal achievement than Brundle had. The fall was harder, too, but Herbert complained to the bitter end that he had suffered as a consequence of the preferential treatment lavished on Schumacher.

He said he was not given sufficient testing, that his car was developed to suit the champion. He felt an 'outcast', and his two wins – his first wins in Formula One – could not wholly compensate for the sense of injustice and mistreatment. He branded Schumacher as 'selfish' yet conceded he could understand such an attitude was part of a champion's make-up. Herbert departed at the end of the year, a sorry figure.

Schumacher says: 'I'm sure Johnny was expecting to be very close to me and wanted to fulfil his dreams. He had never been in a top team and suddenly here he was, he had this opportunity and he thought, "I'm going to be as quick as him". Soon, it became clear he wasn't and he struggled, very much so. Sure, I was upset at some of the things he said about me, but to some degree I could understand his feelings. He needed to protect himself, he wanted to make his situation better than it was.

'I quite often ask myself how I would react in such circumstances. It has not often happened that my team-mate has been quicker than me but when it has I have said, "Okay, he's quick, I need to work". I find a way to change the situation. The car was there for both of us at Benetton. It was not built for me. I used it to the maximum, he did not, and that is the point. Johnny was better in qualifying than he was in the race. He lost even more ground in the race, and that was difficult for him to take.'

When Irvine was awarded the seat next to Schumacher at Ferrari he did not fall into the trap that had snared others. He made no rash promises, no wild predictions. He was the No. 2 and accepted his role. He saw this as a chance to compare himself with the best and he would simply endeavour to be as close to the double champion as possible. The Ulsterman had a reputation for being quick and combative on the track; irreverent, fun-loving and laid-back off it. The early indications were that they could form a sound and productive relationship. They appeared to develop a healthy understanding both professionally and personally.

'Eddie has a way of taking the pressure off himself and putting it on me,' Michael observes. 'I have to say, I would do the same in his position. But I am comfortable with the situation. I am in a position now to be clearer about

Eddie Irvine *(left)* and Schumacher clearly have serious Ferrari business to discuss.

what I can achieve, want to achieve and want to have. He is equally clear about the situation between us and thinks, "If I'm better, fantastic", but what he says is, "If I am within so much of him I can be happy". At the same time, people outside will say, "Yeah, he has achieved what he thought, so he is good".

'He's clever, good fun, and from the start we got on very well together. He is very different from me in certain and obvious respects, but perhaps that helps us in our relationship. Because we are so different we can get close and communicate for the benefit of the team. That is often the case when you have two opposites.'

Prost and Senna had an amicable relationship during their early days together at McLaren, but eventually the rivalry forced them apart. Distrust and envy festered and the ultimate acrimony exposed flaws in their personalities, but they remain pre-eminent in Schumacher's judgement.

Michael says: 'Senna stands out among the drivers I have known in Formula One. Prost also. They both stand out, not only for their achievements but for the individual characters they brought into Formula One. You will only really understand my character after my time racing. I hear people say I am doing it the same way as Senna or the same way as Prost, but I don't think I am. I have achieved things differently, I will continue to achieve things differently, and that will be recognised later, not now.

'In my view what set Senna and Prost apart was the talent they had and the ability to improve the talent better than others do. Other drivers seem unable to always run the car on the limit. They seem sometimes to beat themselves on the limit, and that's the difference. That's why a driver should always be just below his personal limit.

'Prost was gentle with the car. I'm not like Alain. I don't think I am like Ayrton, either, who was aggressive. They were two opposites and I don't really know where I am compared with them. Some suggest I am somewhere between them, but I can't say. We shall have to see later, and judge then.'

The other champion Schumacher competed against in Formula One was Mansell, and Michael says of the Englishman: 'He is in a totally different category again. I don't think you can really compare him with Alain or Ayrton. I think if you go back to the times when Ayrton won his Championships, the circumstances were maybe a bit similar to mine. In my view it's clear I didn't have the best car and was competing against somebody with the best car, and was still able to make it.

'In 1992, when Nigel won his Championship, his Williams was clearly a big step better than Ayrton's McLaren. I think it was also the time of traction control and active suspension, and Riccardo struggled with these things. With a normal, passive car it depends how critical it is, but it is easy to find the limit. Maybe in 1991 Riccardo found it easy and, in the first part of the

Mansell's stunning charge to pole at Silverstone, 1992.

season, was better than Nigel because he was smoother and more consistent. But in 1992 they had a car that was difficult and Riccardo was going through corners not knowing what was going to happen, whereas Nigel just went for it and was a lot quicker.

'Riccardo could not find that extra bit, Nigel could, and that capacity gave Nigel the advantage. I remember Nigel in qualifying at Silverstone that year, producing a one minute 18.9 second lap – absolutely magnificent. I mean, this was unbelievable, and on occasions like that Nigel looked special. I am not sure whether I, or Ayrton, or anyone would have been better than he was on that day. I think when his confidence was not total, then he could struggle, but when he did have total confidence he was able to take another step up.'

Schumacher's decision to leave Benetton for Ferrari precipitated moves in the opposite direction for Jean Alesi and Gerhard Berger, two of the leading drivers seeking Championship fulfilment.

Michael says: 'In terms of sheer speed, I think Alesi is quicker than Berger, but Gerhard is a person who can develop and understands why he is quick. Jean quite often is quick and doesn't know why he is quick. I don't know if Jean's temperament can be a problem for him. It depends to some extent on the people he works with. When Prost was with him he was able to teach Jean and make him work. Who you work with is quite important and Jean could not have better people to work with. But you, as the driver, have to work with them and once you do that they will work with you. If you expect them just to work with you, I don't think it can work. It has to be a two-way operation.

Below left Berger and Schumacher exchange observations in 1995 before exchanging teams.

Below A jubilant and emotional Alesi hitches a lift back to the pits with the champion after his maiden Grand Prix victory at Montreal, 1995.

'There are a lot of drivers with ability in Formula One and that, of course, is the way it should be at this level. Jacques Villeneuve came to Grand Prix racing after winning the IndyCars Championship and was immediately competitive in the Williams, although it was obvious he and Hill had a clear advantage with that car. With drivers such as Rubens Barrichello we are going to have to wait to see the best of them. It is very difficult to name the champions of the future. What we want, above all, is good competition on the track, and good relations off the track.'

Formula One debutant Jacques Villeneuve leads from his Williams team-mate, Hill, at Melbourne, 1996.

Barrichello, driving a Jordan Peugeot, heads Schumacher's Ferrari in the 1996 Brazilian Grand Prix.

The Man behind the Visor

Michael Schumacher has had a phenomenal impact on Formula One in a relatively short time span, but Formula One has left its mark on Michael Schumacher. He fixed his eyes on a photograph of him taken shortly after his Grand Prix debut, in 1991, and smiled resignedly. 'I have certainly changed my hair,' the sleeker Schumacher said.

The expression on the leaner, perhaps harder, face altered as he acknowledged the sport had accelerated the ageing process. 'I have got older a lot quicker during my Formula One career,' he went on. 'And sure, I have changed as a person. I have grown up, and developed myself. Some people think in the right direction, some people the wrong direction, but I have developed the way I wanted to. I have more understanding about people and things.'

Again he glanced at that picture of the young Benetton driver, his countenance as bright as the Camel yellow racesuit. 'A lot of the people who took pictures of me around that time would come back to me a month later and say they wanted to take another picture. Their newspaper said the old pictures were no longer any good to them because I changed every month. I think that was the case, especially during that early part of my Formula One career. I got older quite quickly and yes, the face has changed.

'The person also. I was very careful when I was younger. I tried not to say the wrong things, things I didn't know anything about. So I shut my mouth. But now I say things more openly because I have more idea about things, more confidence.'

If there is one characteristic you would reckon Schumacher never lacked it is confidence. From the very first weekend in Formula One, at Spa, he radiated self-belief, the absolute conviction this was where he belonged. Gerhard Berger believes Schumacher's most potent weapon is his confidence which, the Austrian says, enables him to 'drive through problems'. It would also seem to arm him to drive through the opposition psychologically. This strain of confidence is considered in some quarters to be plain arrogance. Whether such a judgement is the product of envy or objective analysis, it is challenged by the German.

The way he was…

…the way he is.

Schumacher, behind Senna and Mansell, in his short-lived Grand Prix debut, Spa, 1991.

'It would be wrong to say it doesn't hurt me when people say I am arrogant, but it is unfortunately the case that some say this and I realise you cannot expect everybody to like you, or everybody to think the same way. Some drivers like each other, some hate each other. It has always been like this. It is the way with all people. I know what I am like and if I look around me I have reason enough to be confident because the majority of people are behind me. There will always be a group that is not behind you, but as long as this is a small group it's okay.

'Much of this problem is because of the time element. In a very short time I have become very successful, very famous, but that has been too little time for people to really know me. Only a longer period of time will give people the true picture of me. It is difficult for us in Formula One to allow people to know us and understand us. You start hiding yourself away at races because there is not enough time available to give to all the people who want to meet you and know you. In this situation I am a different person to these people than I am to those who really know me.

'The people who know me think differently about me and I am sure the attitude of other people towards me will change as they get to know me as well. I certainly do not feel I am arrogant or cold or all these other things some people say I am. I don't like it when other people are arrogant. I cannot handle that and I wouldn't like to work with arrogant people.

'What I try to be is honest. This is a principle of my life. If you look back through the years, I don't think you will find anything to contradict this. Honesty has always determined my way of working, working together with everybody. In my view this is not only fair but also gives you the best results. You should be open and tell the truth. If you are not prepared to do that then keep your mouth shut.'

Much as some of his team-mates may have complained about the 'favouritism' lavished on Schumacher, they have to concede he has been up front about assuming the benefits and, it should be said, the responsibilities that come with No. 1 status. If you work with him you know where you stand. Eddie Irvine was realistic enough to accept that and bright enough not to say anything that might be construed as questioning the natural order of things. Indeed, Irvine has willingly added his voice to the chorus acclaiming his partner as the best in the sport. That goes down well with Schumacher. Of course he has an ego. So has Irvine. You would be hard pressed to find a driver at this level or an individual at this level of any other sport or profession who does not have an ego that demands to be fed.

What consoles Irvine and others in their relations with Schumacher is the discovery that he is no intellectual. Ross Brawn talked about his intelligence but that was a driving intelligence. His intelligence in matters of the world beyond the race track is inevitably more limited. As he has revealed, he hated school. He was no academic. But his willingness to learn in areas he recognises as important has developed his mind. He felt able to talk at length about France's nuclear testing programme in the South Pacific at the end of

1995, saying he had listened to, and appreciated, the French case. He concluded, however, that he had to denounce the development of weapons. When the Green Party challenged his plan for an indoor kart track in Kerpen he said he would invite them along to see what fun it gave people.

His talent in racing is such and his confidence in that talent is such that he now has a power and superiority he enjoys exerting within Formula One. Perhaps he is indulging himself in topics outside because he has found this vehicle to drive away what was not merely an early lack of confidence, but in fact a social inferiority complex.

The intensity of his decision to immerse himself in Formula One affords scant opportunity for respite or, as Irvine contends, relaxation. Schumacher takes the view this is a serious business and should be treated accordingly, but that he does balance his commitment with relaxation. Even so, is he not a mite too serious? Does he never surrender himself to unbridled fun, to base frivolity?

'Of course I have fun and enjoy myself,' he responds in a tone more like a retort. 'The situation in Formula One is different from the situations earlier in my career. In go-karts and Formula Three, for example, we raced together, went out together and had fun together. Naturally, you miss that. But it is different in Formula One and so much in your life changes with it. Now I

Michael, Corinna and friends at Monaco.

have my fun more with my wife and friends away from the racing. We like to go to musicals and organise things together.

'For example, on my 27th birthday one of my friends phoned me to give me his good wishes, we had a little chat and I asked him to tell another friend I wouldn't be able to go karting as planned because I had cracked a rib skiing. (We'll come back to that later.) He said he would be seeing him later and would tell him. Then the line broke up so I put down the phone. I turned round and the guy was standing in front of me. He was one of a group of nine or ten friends who had come down from Germany. I didn't know anything about it – Corinna had organised a party at our home in Monaco and suddenly there were about 20 people.

'We have a number of parties over the winter and lots of fun. At New Year we have a party with the same group of friends. To welcome 1996 the party was at the home of a friend in Germany and we all ended up in the pool. Fortunately it is an indoor pool, but the year before I was not so fortunate. My friend started to pour drinks over me, I did the same to him and then he started trying to push me into the outdoor pool. Eventually he succeeded but I made sure I took him with me. It was two degrees. C-O-L-D. I had a bad bout of flu after that.

'This is the side of me nobody sees. Nobody, that is, apart from my friends. When I am working I am working, so there is no reason why other people should know about this. I have a very public working life and I value my private life and the time I have away from the public eye. I need this time to relax, to be with my wife and my friends.'

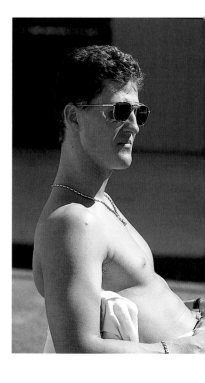

Above and below
Michael showing he can relax sometimes.

One or two from the Formula One fraternity will have witnessed, with some amusement, this lighter side at various end-of-season, or end-of-championship contest, parties. He has been known to be not only the worse for drink but also in possession of a cigarette, although to imply he might have been smoking it might be a slight distortion of the truth. As one observer recalls: 'He looked like a 12-year-old trying a cigarette for the first time. He seemed to be doing rather more blowing than inhaling. It was very funny.'

This quest for privacy has convinced him the tax haven of Monaco – which he has shared with many other Formula One drivers – is not worth the personal cost. He found it virtually impossible to move around the Principality, to his office or the shops, without being besieged by tourists wanting autographs and 'just one picture with little Fritz'. Even the sun, the sea and the boat trips could no longer compensate for the hijacking of his liberty.

He had already taken refuge at Willi Weber's house in France and taken to making trips deep inland, discovering a different kind of beauty and the joys of tranquillity along the valleys of the Maritime Alps. To find tax benefits – although not as favourable as in Monaco – he ventured into Switzerland. At a small village some ten kilometres from Lake Geneva he found a 15-room house, complete with large garden, available for rent and decided to take it. As a new resident he was not allowed to buy his own property but plans to do so in due course.

His four dogs will also doubtless appreciate the move. Jenny, a West

Floh joins the team.

Highland Terrier, was the original girl in his life. He also has a couple of Belgian sheepdogs, Bonny and Tracey, which had stayed with Weber, and a creature of dubious pedigree. Corinna fell for the apparent stray on their trip to Sao Paulo for the 1996 Brazilian Grand Prix, had it cleansed of its squatter fleas and, at a reported cost of around £3,000, flew it back to Europe and a canine paradise on earth. It is now called 'Floh', which means flea. They also took in two cats – and called them Mosley and Ecclestone!

'My wife and I love walking with our dogs,' Michael says. 'That is when I find true relaxation. I love natural beauty – sunrise, sunsets, the stars. I love the countryside, the peace and the quiet. It is so different from Formula One and so important to me.'

Now wouldn't you know it? The man makes millions only to realise the best things in life are free. Cynicism, and jealousy, flow all too easily, but hear him out.

'After you have a certain amount of money it no longer has the same meaning. For me the money means security for the future and independence. I have this and I appreciate it. Time is freedom for me, not the money itself. That is why I have my own plane. It enables me to be a lot more flexible and so save more time.'

He has a Challenger, a nine-seater jet capable of flying inter-continental and saving him days and incalculable hassle over the course of a hectic annual racing and testing schedule. If this seems an extreme and extravagant

Michael with one of his toys – the Ducati Monster.

Michael and Corinna – leaving it all behind.

length to go to just for a walk with the dogs, bear in mind the relative drain on his income is considerably less than the average family car is on the average family man.

Unlike some past Grand Prix high-fliers, Schumacher has no inclination to pilot his plane. 'I have no interest in learning that,' he says. 'It is good to have it, to fly from A to B as quickly and simply as possible, but that is the end of my interest. I might be more interested in piloting a helicopter, but that would be for the future.'

Flying lessons take time and time, as he stresses, is too precious to trade lightly. Similarly, he has been reluctant to organise Italian lessons. Besides, his endeavours to learn French almost blew his mind and English, which he has pretty well mastered, is the motor racing language. Michael's other 'toys' include two Ferraris, a Mercedes, the obligatory four-wheel drive number, a Renault Traffic to transport his karts, a Sunseeker boat and a couple of motor bikes.

To his boyhood recreations of football, tennis and swimming Schumacher the affluent man has added skiing. 'I didn't ski when I was young because we did not have the money to go on skiing holidays. This was something I got into later and really enjoyed. I ski in the winter, no later than the middle of January, so that if I have an accident I have time to recover before the beginning of the season. Again, I believe if I do it within my limits nothing

Geared up for the slopes with
Johnny Herbert.

is going to happen unless there is some unforeseen thing which you cannot
prevent. It would be fairly stupid to go skiing a week before the first race.'

He went skiing at the end of 1995 in Norway to avoid the over-
enthusiastic attention he had encountered on the Alpine slopes as well as in
Monaco. 'It was quieter, for sure, but very cold – minus 30 degrees. You had
to cover your face to protect yourself from the cold. But we had heated boots
and otherwise it was okay. I tried longer skis and got on really quite well with
them. I think they suited me.'

But what about the cracked rib?

'Oh, I had a little accident, but nothing too serious. In fact, I was testing
again just a couple of weeks later. It certainly didn't affect my work.'

Heiner Büchinger

The extraordinary salary Schumacher commands for working as a racing driver is at least matched by what he earns from personal sponsorship and endorsements, and his own marketing venture, the Michael Schumacher Collection. You can buy anything from cups and umbrellas to bath robes and leather jackets, a total of 220 articles and souvenirs bearing the Michael Schumacher Collection logo, which features the silhouette of a racing car, and help boost turnover from $50 million in 1995 to a projected $100 million in 1996.

Schumacher says: 'I have always been interested in this possibility. Ayrton was the one who saw the potential of starting his own marketing organisation, and he developed the idea. I felt I should do it because I really hate it when other people make money from my name. I don't see why anyone else should go around making money because of my success when they have nothing to do with me. So we took this step and Willi Weber has done a very good job on it. We have had to spend a lot of money getting it together but I think we have now found the right level with the business.'

Weber heads the ever expanding commercial operation and team of employees. It is also a measure of Schumacher's stature that he has a full-time press officer, a big, bearded, affable German called Heiner Büchinger, who organises his interviews and provides a regular flow of information to the media. Much as Michael is protective of his wealth and earning capacity, he is known to be generous to charitable causes. He has made substantial contributions to UNESCO, rationalising they are the experts and it is their job to know where the money is needed. The photographic rights at his wedding were sold for charity.

Sponsors' engagements and television appearances are part of the working schedule.

He also, along with a number of other leading drivers, gives of his time to the running of the Grand Prix Drivers' Association, which was regenerated after the deaths of Ratzenberger and Senna, and works with various safety and planning commissions established by FIA following the tragedies.

However misunderstood he may feel, this proud, focused man is not one to overtly canvas popularity. The love of the masses is not his motivation. When, therefore, he joined Ferrari at the expense of the fans' kindred spirit, the passionate, volatile, vulnerable Jean Alesi, and received a cool reception, Schumacher made no stage-managed attempt to assuage them. Utterly Teutonic, he would have no truck with the forced, empty gesture; he had no time for soppy, sentimental rhetoric. If he was to win them over he would do so with his performances on the track. In this respect he had more in common with the steely Niki Lauda than Alesi or that most revered Ferrarista, Gilles Villeneuve. Neither Villeneuve nor Alesi won a

Above left and right
Savouring another victory at Spa with his fans… and Jean.

Championship for the Italians. Lauda won two. Schumacher has maintained the same attitude in his dealings with the infamous Italian Press and, well into his first season at Maranello, peace and good relations appeared to flourish. He seeks respect for the man and driver he is.

'I am aware of my deficiencies,' he says. 'I am not perfect, nobody is. I am trying all the time to improve as a person. I am working on this, so the public can understand me better. But I can only be Michael Schumacher and be honest about that.'

Martin Brundle, one of the sport's more perceptive and astute protagonists, proffers this image of his former team-mate: 'He is refreshingly down to earth. He's got his feet on the ground. He's got values, family values. He's close to his parents and does all he can to help his kid brother's racing. I've got a lot of time for him as a person, as well as a driver.'

Schumacher's values and morals were examined early in his Formula One career. The young, fresh, untainted star-in-the-making would inevitably have temptation put his way, but he was aghast when the subtle advances of a mature female television reporter in the back of a taxi became an overt proposition. He recoiled and exclaimed: 'You're old enough to be my mother!'

He has consistently indicated he does not plan driving far into the next millennium, and Brundle suspects he will stick to his word. 'Schuey knows where he's going, what he wants and how to go about it. I don't think he's the kind who'll hang around. He'll do it and get out. That's the way he is.'

Despite the closeness of the family – or probably because of it – Schumacher has always been uneasy about having his parents at the Grands Prix. 'If they are there I am thinking about them, feel responsible for them, and feel obliged to spend time with them. But if I do that I cannot give myself totally to the work,' he explained. When Corinna goes along she studiously keeps a low profile and permits her husband the concentration he insists on.

And yet, for all his professional devotion, Michael's greatest ambition is strictly a family affair. 'More than anything we want to have children' he said. And how would Michael react if his child wanted to follow in his tyre tracks? 'I have an open mind on that, it would be entirely up to him – or her. They will have to live their own lives and make their own decisions.'

At the 1996 Italian Grand Prix, Michael announced that Corinna was expecting their first child the following Spring, 'It is the most wonderful feeling,' said the glowing father-to-be. 'Racing is one thing, but this is quite another.'

Man behind the visor.

The Challenge of Ferrari

Through the summer of 1995 it became increasingly evident that Benetton would be unable to hold on to their much-coveted No. 1 driver beyond that season. Flavio Briatore submitted to the inevitable by publicly, as well as privately, courting Jean Alesi. The great crusade had run its course. Schumacher would take with him a second drivers' title and leave them with their first Constructors' Championship. It was the perfect finale, the fairytale ending. Briatore graciously bade farewell with the declaration: 'Michael has become the greatest driver in the world and next year he will still be the greatest driver in the world.'

Schumacher departed with mixed emotions, but for all the sadness of the farewells he was driven by the yearning for a new challenge. 'I had four and a half years with Benetton,' he explains. 'Fantastic times, a lot of success. We achieved everything and I didn't feel I could go on in new directions with them. And that's what I wanted. I wanted to do new things, I wanted to have new targets, new motivation and develop myself.'

Benetton would sign Alesi and then Gerhard Berger, the other exile from Ferrari, but whither this new direction for Schumacher? Unsurprisingly, Williams were interested but, as their technical director, Patrick Head, subsequently stated, the asking price was beyond their reach. Besides, the best driver in the best car would not have been the best equation for the show, and it would be naive to imagine the hand of Bernie Ecclestone was not involved in the orchestration of movements. McLaren and their engine partners, Mercedes, would certainly have welcomed the German, but that was not the direction that lured him. The path he chose led to Italy and the most famous, revered name in motor racing: Ferrari.

That fame and reverence, however, had been built on achievements long past and it seemed the hold on the faithful now had more to do with mythology than fact. For Ferrari read Team Italia; a compulsion, a commitment, a source of passion and torment. There is no parallel in motor sport. They had not had the drivers' champion since 1979 and last won the Constructors' Championship in 1983. Here was the challenge, perhaps the ultimate challenge – to make Ferrari champions again.

Opposite Emotion Italian style.

It would, of course, be naive also to imagine money was not a factor in the move and it is understood the two-year contract Schumacher signed with Ferrari was worth $50 million. 'I want to be paid what reflects the work I am doing,' he says. He maintains he could have earned more elsewhere – presumably at McLaren Mercedes. It now mattered little anyway. He had entered the realms of fantasy money, figures beyond the comprehension of the ordinary man. Financial concerns had been consigned to history; the racing challenge beckoned.

'I really feel this has given me the new motivation I wanted,' he says. 'I have come to a team that hasn't had a Formula One world champion for 17 years, and if I can do it here I will know I haven't done it at just one team but two teams, and the second a supposedly difficult team with difficult circumstances.'

Schumacher's enthusiasm was not shared by Ferrari fans en masse. Many lamented the ousting of Alesi, some even angered. They regarded the French-Sicilian as one of their own: emotional, devoted, mercurial. Schumacher was perceived as cool and distant. What's more, he made no attempt to persuade them otherwise. It was simply not in his nature to throw himself into the embrace of strangers. He wanted their respect and support, and nothing more. It was not a snub; this was the way he was. The way he is.

He made no pretence of a life-long dream to drive for Ferrari. 'I certainly never had any thoughts or fantasies about that,' he says. 'I knew nothing about Ferrari when I was young. Remember, it was never even a passion for me to become a Formula One driver at all. Ferrari is another story altogether. I wouldn't even have dreamt about this.'

Michael was equally adamant he had no dreams of delivering the Championship to Maranello in his first season. 'I try to be realistic all the time and I am trying to be realistic when I say we cannot expect to win the Championship in '96 but hope to in '97. I will be satisfied if we are competitive and compete for wins in the middle and later stages of the first season. If we win two or three races we will fulfil our expectations.

'I have always been a person to play down things, and if we achieve more everyone is happy. I don't see any sense in changing that philosophy. First of all, I believe we are going to have certain problems. That is logical. We have got to get to know each other, to understand each other, and then learn how to work together. That will take time. It took me four and a half years to achieve what I achieved at Benetton and I cannot expect to do all of this in three months at Ferrari. Certainly my target is to win the Championship and I have made a choice which I think can give me the success I am looking for in the long term. I feel Ferrari is going the right way and they are not missing that much to be successful.'

The general view was that if Ferrari could not get it right with Schumacher they never would. Even Gianni Agnelli, the patriarch of the Fiat empire, acknowledged as much. Little wonder, therefore, the team were

Man and machine.

prepared to meet not only his financial demands but also his demands on working practice. That meant the operation would be focused on Schumacher, as it had been at Benetton, that he would undertake as much of the testing as he deemed necessary and that the No. 2 driver, Eddie Irvine, would have to take what was given him.

Winter testing confirmed the parameters and, Schumacher asserted, reinforced his belief he had taken the correct direction. He was instantly quick in the 1995 car – evidence, he suggested, he did not depend upon a car created specially for him, a privilege Damon Hill and others reckoned he enjoyed at Benetton. 'I don't expect to have a car built specially to my style. I get a car from the designer, this time John Barnard, and from this base we try to make it fit into my style.'

Many were surprised at the apparent ease with which Schumacher was able to fit into the Ferrari team. There again, perhaps it was more a case of their fitting around him. Whichever way you look at it, there was a fresh urgency and sense of purpose in the camp. Benetton personnel will tell you of the motivation he generated through the ranks there. Now it was happening here at Ferrari. And not because he bullied them. This was no ogre but a regular guy with an irregular talent and dedication.

Schumacher appreciated a budget which permitted development by trial and error. Lengthy meetings to consider the most logical course had been the customary procedure at Benetton. 'Here I am involved in the development all the time and that actually helps take away the pressure.'

The man under most pressure at a car launch is the designer and at Maranello on 15th February, 1996, John Barnard looked on anxiously as his latest offering, the F310, the first Ferrari racing car to be powered by a V10 engine, was unveiled. Some months earlier the Englishman, who works from a base in Surrey, had expressed his enthusiasm about the prospect of having his car driven by Schumacher, and now his usual caution gave way to declarations of 'optimism'. Schumacher said he was impressed but warned that reliability would be a key to Ferrari's season.

The F310 was heralded as 'radical' yet some observers were surprised Barnard had not gone for a raised nose, while others wondered whether it was necessary to produce a 'bathtub' of a cockpit to comply with new safety regulations. Teething problems, particularly with the gearbox, also served to restrain the traditional pre-season surge of expectation. Come the opening round of the World Championship, at the new Australian Grand Prix venue of Melbourne, it was clear Ferrari, even with Schumacher at the wheel, were no match for Williams.

Schumacher had the unusual and unexpected experience of being out-qualified by his team-mate but, after a series of problems, was content enough with fourth place on the grid. Hill, the Championship favourite, was also beaten by his partner, the French-Canadian, Jacques Villeneuve, who would therefore start his first Formula One race from pole position.

Irvine dutifully allowed Schumacher through to carry the fight to Williams but it was a forlorn bid. He had to retire with brake failure after losing fluid, leaving the Ulsterman to collect a creditable third place behind Hill and Villeneuve. Williams' success further fuelled complaints they had been 'too liberal' in their interpretation of the cockpit rules. However, FIA determined the cars legal and now Ferrari and the rest were aware of the scale of their task.

Schumacher said: 'The fact that we were able to stay in front of Benetton shows a big step already. But the car is still not there. This race was more or less a test. Nevertheless, the car was much better during the race.'

It transpired that the new, slimline titanium gearbox on the F310 was not quite ready for that step. Technicians discovered hairline cracks in it after the Australian race and the team decided to revert to the 1995 rear-end for the Grands Prix in South America.

The bumpy Interlagos circuit, in Brazil, proved unforgiving territory for the Ferrari and Schumacher had to dig deep into his resources of willpower to take fourth place on the grid again. 'The car is so bad you would not believe it,' he said. This time Hill was on pole and this time his victory, in the rain, was never in doubt. He had the additional satisfaction of lapping his old adversary, who at least finished third after a stoic performance to make his first appearance on the podium as a Ferrari driver. But his glum features indicated that was scant consolation.

Undaunted, Schumacher wrestled the twitchy Ferrari to second place on the grid in Argentina and doggedly tracked Hill's Williams in the early part of the race only for flying debris to damage his rear wing and eventually he had to abandon the chase. 'I feel I would have finished not that far from Damon,' he said, 'but I don't believe I could have beaten him.'

Hill had launched his campaign with three straight wins and was moved to say: 'It can't get any better than this, can it?' Even so, the Englishman still had not moved Schumacher to rank him among his six 'most naturally talented drivers', excluding, of course, himself. The champion nominated, for the benefit of a German newspaper, in no particular order: Jean Alesi, Mika Hakkinen, Eddie Irvine, Heinz-Harald Frentzen, Rubens Barrichello and Mika Salo. Schumacher reasons: 'Damon Hill has improved a lot. He's a very good racing driver. But he tends to make mistakes under pressure. I think the reason might be that he did not have a lot of experience before he came into Formula One. Most drivers who do have a better view of what is better in a fight.'

Prophetic words. Hill's tardy start in the Grand Prix of Europe, at the Nurburgring, exposed him to rather more scrapping than he anticipated and he could finish no higher than fourth. Not that Schumacher was able to repeat the stupendous success of the previous season here. Much as he hustled the Ferrari, he could not prevent Villeneuve's maiden Formula One win and had to accept second place.

Ferrari president,
Luca di Montezemolo.

John Barnard.

'All the time I was thinking about last year's race, when I was catching Alesi in the last few laps,' Michael said. 'I was hoping that maybe a situation would come in which I could get past Jacques, as I did Jean. But Jacques drove a fantastic race, and he also had the edge on top speed, so there was no way for me to pass him.'

The tinge of disappointment could not be camouflaged and it showed also on the face of the Ferrari president, Luca di Montezemolo, giving the cameras the full range of expressions from the pit wall. This had, however, hauled back a modicum of credibility for the Scuderia and their flamboyant figurehead. He, in turn, took the opportunity to profess his loyalty to Barnard, the distant designer being subjected to another wave of criticism in the Italian media.

Di Montezemolo allowed Barnard to stay in England because he had no alternative, but now he begged a little something in return. 'John is British and sometimes does not understand the Italian Press. I am happy to have him with me. I hope he understands that Italy is not so far from England. It's up to you to interpret that. What I want is to win. I try to put my people in the best position to work – hire Schumacher, go for the 10-cylinder engine, putting John in the wind tunnel last year without pushing him to come to races. Now I need something back.'

Right on cue, his No. 1 driver provided it. 'For me,' the president said, 'Michael means something very important, just as Ayrton Senna was to McLaren and Niki Lauda was to Ferrari in the 1970s.'

The comparisons recur: not only exceptional talent but also the strength of leadership to carry the entire team. And nowhere was that strength, that character and resolve and resilience, more necessary than at Ferrari. Even Alain Prost, winner of four World Championships and more Grands Prix than any other driver, did not have the strength to meet the unique challenge of Maranello. Some close to the hallowed legacy of Enzo Ferrari, however, were beginning to wonder whether Schumacher had been given licence to exert too much strength. Who was really running the operation? Who was governing the test schedules? And should not a team of Ferrari's stature have two frontline drivers? Others pointed to the rejuvenation of the camp, the new sense of optimism running through the ranks. The final judgement, as always, would be based on results.

For the first time, an Italian race crowd would be able to judge the progress so far. Imola and the San Marino Grand Prix were next. Schumacher sought to douse the inevitable flames of expectation by playing down his prospects – then set the Autodromo Enzo e Dino Ferrari alight with a scintillating lap to claim his first pole with the Prancing Horse. Hill, thus relegated to second spot on the grid, confessed it felt like 'a punch in the stomach'.

The Championship leader need not have been anxious. The modifications to the F310 were still not effective enough to enable it to compete with the

Williams in the race and Hill was a comfortable winner from Schumacher. The German said: 'Before coming here I would have thought second place was impossible for us because Imola is so bumpy and our car has not worked so well on bumps. But actually it was perfect from the beginning, although not fast enough to run with the Williams. Not yet, anyway.'

The following race, however, held out the promise of not merely running with the Williams but actually beating it. Monaco was the preserve of the very best drivers. For a generation it had been dominated by three men: Prost, Senna (with a record six wins) and Schumacher. The new monarch, having reigned for two seasons, was in no mood to abdicate now and testing had encouraged him to stray from his recent, cautious path. 'I always try to stay on the ground with my predictions, but I could see a victory in Monaco.'

This new course seemed justified when Michael took pole, although a celebratory wave to the gallery on his slowing down lap was not appreciated by Gerhard Berger. The Austrian, still trying to improve his qualifying position, had to jump on the brakes to avoid hitting the Ferrari filling the road ahead of him, spun and flashed by the now alert champion – backwards. Schumacher eventually managed to placate a fuming Berger with an apology and acceptance of responsibility.

Alas for Michael and his ever more expectant fan club, he had cause to be contrite again barely half a lap into the race. Left behind by Hill at the start, he tried too hard to make amends and crashed into the barrier. 'I'm upset with myself,' he said. 'It was clearly my fault. It always hurts more when you make a mistake yourself. I'm upset because for the first time I could have won for the team. It is my biggest disappointment in racing.' And then, as if to reassure those with any doubts, he added: 'I AM human.'

It was a day for the unexpected, not to say the bizarre. Only three cars finished, the first of them a Ligier Mugen Honda, driven by the Frenchman, Olivier Panis. A sense of normality would return in Spain, Schumacher qualifying third, behind the Williams pair, and hoping for nothing better in the race. 'I feel this gives a clear picture of the current situation from a technical point of view. Today I got the absolute maximum out of the car. The gap stems mainly from aerodynamic reasons. There is nothing wrong with the engine. Realistically the best I can hope for tomorrow is a podium finish.'

But then he had not accounted for a dramatic change in the weather on race day and the chance to test his skills on a level playing field. Torrential rain greeted the cars on the starting grid at the Circuit de Catalunya, hurling down its challenge to the best racing drivers in the world. Two hours later, the rain would beat its homage to one man apart from the rest. There are moments across the spectrum of human endeavour that seize the senses and freeze in history. To those towering performances in sport we could now add Schumacher's mastery of fellow man and the elements in the 1996 Spanish Grand Prix.

Before it all went wrong, Monaco 1996.

His total domination in conditions that had the others on tenterhooks – Hill went out after a third spin – moved veteran Formula One watchers to compare the performance with Senna's at Donington in 1993 and at Estoril in 1985, as well as Jackie Stewart's at the old Nurburgring, in 1968. A slight misfire was simply another inconvenience to be wafted away with the rain, the spray and the cold.

'It's amazing,' he said at the end, his teeth chattering. 'I wouldn't have bet a penny on it. I don't know why, but the car was perfect and the nature of the circuit just suited it. There were three or four points on the circuit which were critical, with panels of water.'

That water caught out others, but Schumacher sailed serenely through. After another awful start, which had him jostling with the midfield sloggers as the leaders threatened to stretch out beyond reach, he completed the first lap in sixth place. On the 12th lap he went past Villeneuve's Williams to take the lead. 'He just left me standing,' the Canadian admitted. Schumacher pulled clear at the rate of up to four seconds a lap; to a place alone and into our consciousness for ever. It was a maiden victory at the wheel of a Ferrari to defy the imagination of the wildest romantic.

It was also a victory which confirmed opinions, and fears, among present and past members of the Formula One fraternity. Derek Warwick, a former Grand Prix driver, watched Schumacher's demonstration at Barcelona and said: 'I was in awe of the guy... but no-one else is in his league. When I was in Formula One there were always three or four great drivers – Piquet, Prost,

Mansell, Senna and so on. Now there's only one great driver, and that's sad for Formula One.'

Could it be that one great driver is the greatest, greater even than Senna? 'Oh, I don't know about that,' Warwick replied. 'I don't want to agree with that.'

Few want to and we understand why. Death has rendered Senna's memory and stature sacrosanct. Perhaps when Schumacher's career is over it will be possible to make a rational, unemotional assessment of these two extraordinary men. Perhaps not, even then. This much can be claimed: that Schumacher at 27 looks a more complete driver than Senna at the same age. The German appears less vulnerable – though not impervious – to pressure and criticism. The Brazilian could be one moment cold and calculating, the next volatile and illogical. 'The pity,' Warwick added, 'is that they are not both driving for Williams today.' Ah, the ultimate.

A current Grand Prix driver who patently has a problem acknowledging Schumacher's supremacy is Berger, significantly another omitted from the German's list of 'most naturally talented drivers'. The Austrian argued: 'It is always a bit difficult to say who is the best because maybe there is someone at Minardi who is the best and you don't know. But he has some very good strengths and I would say the best quality he has is his confidence. If you have so much success when you are so young, you get this extra bit from the confidence.'

Berger, a former team-mate of Senna, went on: 'I'm not sure it's a good thing to drive through a problem with the car, as Michael does. Long term it is best to sort out the car. Ayrton did occasionally drive through problems, but he had the right mixture. He could drive through and sort out problems. Each person has weak points and maybe Michael has, but I don't like to talk about this. Everyone has weak points.'

By Schumacher's own admission, he still makes mistakes and some contend he can, at times, be a mite too tough on his equipment, or too sure of himself, but Jean Todt, the Ferrari team director, prefers to accentuate the positive. The little Frenchman's admiration for his senior driver has grown through their first working year together. 'He is a fantastic driver and we try to give him the car he deserves,' Todt says. 'He is the best I have worked with, not only his ability but the work he puts into it. He never stops working. The testing he does is incredible.'

From the top management to the humblest mechanic, they all appreciated Schumacher's talent and effort. He had brought them closer together and filled them with hope. It appeared he had struck up a good relationship also with the much feared Italian Press. And now, in classic Ferrari style, that bond and belief were about to be examined through a wretched mid-season period.

Todt had already warned: 'This is not the time to talk of the dawning of a new age.' Schumacher, too, offered a sobering perspective, saying he could

The media hanging on to his every word.

not rate Barcelona his greatest win because he could not explain why he won so convincingly, that the conditions and relative settings of the cars had clouded the contest. Hill, for example, had stated he chose the wrong set-up. All right, so Michael was joint second with Villeneuve in the Championship, and there was talk of a threat to Hill, but hadn't he said all along the title would be an unrealistic target for this year? Even so, none of this circumspection can have prepared him for what was to come.

Schumacher had the new, raised nose on his Ferrari in Canada, which he reckoned was worth one to two-tenths of a second a lap, and he was narrowly squeezed into third place on the grid by Hill and Villeneuve. All that effort was forfeited when the team were unable to start the F310's engine for the formation lap and he had to start at the back of the grid. Despite brake problems, he worked his way up to seventh, only to shed his driveshaft as he accelerated from a pit stop. Irvine had retired on the second lap with a broken pushrod. Hill went on to win from Villeneuve and Schumacher said: 'I think the Championship is nearly decided. It's clearly Damon's year.'

It looked clearer still for Damon after the French Grand Prix – and even gloomier for Ferrari. Elation over Schumacher's pole was blown asunder, along with his engine, on the formation lap. Irvine, relegated to the back of the grid because of technical irregularities, fared little better. He was halted after five laps by a gearbox failure.

'At first I was angry,' Schumacher said. 'Angry above all because in a few seconds I saw all the hard work I had done together with the team go up in smoke. But I have calmed down now. It is at times like these that you must control your emotions and stay cool and rational.'

Not everyone could take it so well. The house of Maranello was pelted with verbal rotten tomatoes, most of them aimed specifically at Todt, who described it as 'the blackest day of my long career in motor sport'. He was reported to have responded with what amounted to an offer of resignation. As he later explained, what he actually said was that if he was asked to leave he would have to. He was less irritated by that misinterpretation than by accusations that the biggest budget in Formula One was being squandered. 'It makes me angry and is completely wrong,' he snapped, going on to argue that, unlike other teams, Ferrari had also to absorb the cost of producing their own engine. In any case, it was just another stormy chapter in the Scuderia saga. It would pass. Wouldn't it?

Hill's win extended his Championship advantage over Villeneuve to 25 points and sufficiently buoyed his confidence to ask Williams for a 1997 contract worth 12 million. Whether that was pounds or dollars depended on which source you trusted. Arriving at Silverstone for the British Grand Prix, a relaxed and mischievous Schumacher was asked if he thought his old rival was worth it. 'Lire?' he could not resist querying. He did also concede the Englishman would be worthy of the title, but added it was merely going out on loan and would return to its rightful owner the following year.

The smile was wiped off Michael's face as, for the third consecutive race, the Ferrari production was reduced to a farce, a tragi-comedy that turned derision into ridicule. This time Schumacher's car lasted three laps before it was retired, a loss of hydraulic pressure in the gearbox leaving it stuck in sixth. Irvine managed five laps until a broken differential bearing ended his day. The cartoonists were made up. The Prancing Horse was portrayed as an old nag, bound for the knacker's yard. In Germany, Schumacher/Ferrari jokes were all the rage. For example:

Michael returns home one evening and tells Corinna he has good news and bad news.

'What's the good news?'

'I'm having a new car next year'

'What's the bad news?'

'It's a Ferrari.'

Again, Schumacher had a dignified reaction to the unending torment. 'This is absurd, but in racing things like this can happen, even if it seems very strange. To go through similar situations like this for three races in a row is more frustrating for the team than it is for me. After Magny-Cours we tested at Monza and Imola with satisfactory results and covered a high mileage without any problems. It is often the case that little things cause the biggest dramas. But together we must overcome this difficult moment and we will succeed.'

Such restraint, if not blind faith, earned Schumacher commendations not only within the embattled Ferrari camp but also at large. A survey in Germany confirmed his image had been enhanced during a season which was destined to cost him the Championship. Not a trendy, pop star image, though, more a decent, upright young man image. Much as he is conscious of his worth, and demands the other benefits of his status, he is a team player, a loyal colleague. Far from seeking to exercise a get-out clause in his contract, he was discussing an extension of his agreement to the end of 1998. He had entered this alliance with his eyes wide open and was determined to see it through.

Another massive, partisan crowd welcomed Michael back to Hockenheim and fourth place at least gave them the chance to wave their flags to the finish, but the F310 was woefully off the pace and Irvine's gearbox failure underlined the team's plight. Hill made up for his blank at Silverstone with the 20th win of his career, so equalling Schumacher's total, and left for a holiday with a 21-point lead in the Championship.

Irvine was thwarted by similar problems at the Hungaroring, but Schumacher was on course for the podium, albeit behind Villeneuve and Hill, when he parked his car, seven laps from the end. He explained: 'The throttle was getting stiff and tended to stick open. Then even the gearbox began to play up. Approaching the slower corners the only way I could slow down was by turning off the cut-out switch to kill the engine and then switch

Pulling away from Villeneuve, Spa 1996.

it on again. But at one point I made a mistake and hit the neutral selector switch and the engine cut out and would not fire up again.'

That lapse finally eliminated Schumacher from the title equation and another Williams one-two sealed for the British team an eighth Constructors' Championship, equalling Ferrari's record. But while Hill and Villeneuve would decide the drivers' title, Schumacher felt he had much to gain from the final quarter of the season. Next up was Spa and, as we have seen, he had an affinity with the place. Remarkable debut, first, second, first (but disqualified), and first in five visits is some record. It must be something in the water. Or else the fact that this is the absolute, authentic driver's circuit.

Rain duly intervened during qualifying, leaving Schumacher third on the grid, behind Villeneuve and Hill. By the first corner, however, the Ferrari had split the Williams and Schumacher was able to stay with Villeneuve. The appearance of the safety car following an accident involving Verstappen's Footwork Hart coincided with Michael's scheduled first pit stop and by the time the confused Williams team had sorted themselves out, the scarlet machine was tucked in behind the McLarens of Coulthard and Hakkinen, in position to assume the lead when they made their stops.

Villeneuve could still have regained the initiative after his second stop yet although he re-emerged just ahead of Schumacher the Ferrari had the greater momentum and shot in front. Villeneuve closed and harried, but Schumacher was unruffled and eventually the chase was abandoned. Now it was three wins here.

'It's like Hollywood life,' Schumacher enthused. 'I thought after my accident on Friday (which cost him a sore knee) that it might be a good omen like last year, when I qualified 16th and won. Even so, I did not expect this because we were so far behind Williams in qualifying. Spa is particularly lucky for me. Perhaps it is because I can use my potential here. There are more high speed corners and that's why I particularly like this circuit. It's especially nice to win when you are not winning so often.'

On the podium he celebrated his second victory for Ferrari and the 21st of his Formula One career with characteristic gusto, pointedly embracing and sharing the joy with Todt. In a quieter moment, Michael said of his team boss: 'It is very rare in Formula One you find real human beings, and he is one of them. He is one of the best things that has happened to Ferrari. I am very happy to be working with him. He has come in for some criticism but that is normal for anyone at the top.'

Any criticism of Schumacher related to his domination within the team (effectively, if very effectively, Scuderia Schumacher) to the exclusion, it was feared in some Italian quarters, of a competitive second driver. They aspire to the Constructors' Championship as well as the drivers' title in future seasons and no less a source than Agnelli prompted speculation that Irvine might be dropped for 1997 by remarking on the talent of Hakkinen, whose contract with McLaren was to expire at the end of the year. As an experienced observer of Ferrari affairs pointed out, Agnelli was not noted for making gratuitous statements.

Schumacher put the case for keeping Irvine to a huddle of Italian journalists, arguing the benefits of continuity and understanding. Besides, he said, he had had a number of good team-mates and been quicker than all of them. 'I could try to slow down,' he suggested with a grin and heavy sarcasm.

How about Ralf, his younger brother, who had made a favourable impression during a test drive in a McLaren Mercedes? 'That would be unfair in his first season,' Michael said. 'He needs to be given time, then maybe in the future we might get together. We'll see.' Ralf would follow Michael's course by signing for Jordan, who had accepted a financial settlement with their original 'Schumi' over his switch to Benetton.

Michael's team-mate was thought to be one of the 'other details' under discussion in the negotiations for a contract in 1998. He insisted money was not an issue. He was reported to have been seeking an increase of up to $10 million on his current deal. But then money did not appear to be an issue with Ferrari, either. Agnelli had said before this race: 'He deserves to have more money for driving such a car.'

Now the media were hanging on to Schumacher's every word and he took no heed of the mobile phone ringing in the pocket of an Italian reporter. 'Pronto... Si.'

It's for you,' the reporter said, pressing the phone into Michael's hand. 'It's the president.'

'Hello... thanks... my pleasure.'

'He's unbelievable,' Schumacher said, handing back the phone. 'You don't see the president of another company being so interested in Formula One.'

There again, it is difficult to envisage another president like Luca di Montezemolo and another company like Ferrari, and, after a summer of discontent, this was an opportunity too good to miss for the PR-conscious di Montezemolo. The suddenly changing mood was likely to become rampant euphoria over the following two weeks, reaching a frenzied climax of anticipation at the Italian Grand Prix. Schumacher realised as much and the concern became evident in his countenance.

'I am quite worried about Monza,' he said. 'Especially after winning this race. Expectations will be high. I feel a little uneasy. I'm not sure we'll be able to do the same job as here. I'm afraid we'll not be as competitive. The people then become hysterical if things go wrong. Please,' he exhorted the Italian journalists, 'keep it calm, keep it calm.'

He should have known they could not. Almost a full season with Ferrari ought to have told him that and, deep down, he must have known that. It was reasonable to assume Monza would be bedlam. An appropriate juncture, therefore, to reflect on his Ferrari adventure so far.

'I expected more problems early in the season but I believe we were lucky then. We have had more problems later than I expected. I wanted to be more

The next Schumacher –
younger brother Ralf.

competitive towards the end of the season and at least we have won two races, which I hoped for, and overall we have reason to be happy. You can see the developments and the team is getting stronger the more we work together.'

Schumacher had used a seven-speed gearbox at Spa, another product of the development programme. The new car – said to bear a distinct resemblance to the Williams – was due to be ready by Christmas and be put through a comprehensive test schedule in readiness for 1997. The technical side is one thing. How about the human side? 'It is always like this in life,' he said philosophically. 'There are good things and not so good things. I feel people are giving me respect but they are so emotional. They lose control. They like to kiss you and take you.'

He had disconcerting proof. At a test an admirer had an apparently irresistible compulsion to lunge at Schumacher as he posed for photographers and planted a kiss on him. 'He could at least have shaved. It wouldn't have been so bad if it was a girl.'

But have not the Germans also gone wild for him? At this race they turned up in their scores of thousands, as they had elsewhere throughout Europe, spreading their camp-sites across the Ardennes landscape as never before. We had known Mansell mania, we had seen Senna's devoted disciples all around the world, yet nothing like this. Here was a phenomenon that had given cult following another dimension.

'Yes,' he reluctantly conceded, 'also Germans, but not in the same way. I am not sure of Italians.'

This, remember, was the man who did not court the public in the blatant manner others had. He enjoyed the support, and self-evidently revelled in it. Hero-worship, however, was another matter and he found that difficult to cope with. He recoils when people touch and grab him. He craves just to be one of the people yet knows it is no longer possible. That is why he reluctantly agrees to the attendance of minders when they are deemed absolutely necessary and why his traditional 'impromptu' walk into the woods at Spa to meet his fans has become a stage-managed production. For all that he was content to be locked into the Ferrari cause – and braced himself for Monza.

By the time they reached that great sporting cathedral, just north of Milan, the self-styled gods of Formula One were re-locating some of their subjects. Hill had revealed his sacking by Williams, who in turn announced his place would go to Frentzen. We were reminded of Schumacher's statement, at the beginning of the year, that he would have been less confident with someone else in the Williams.

Now he said: 'I hope I have a car good enough to compete with Heinz-Harald. Now he has the chance to show what he can do. We had good, close racing before and I hope we can again. I don't know how good it is for Damon. I think we will now see what he is really like. It is an opportunity for him to prove he is better than some people think and maybe surprise them.'

Frentzen stated: 'I think Frank Williams signed me because he wants me to beat Michael next year', which implied Hill was not considered capable of handling that task once Schumacher had his competitive Ferrari. Here, at the 1996 Italian Grand Prix, the task looked under Hill's control after he beat Villeneuve and Schumacher to pole and then, with a rare demonstration of aggression, fought off a surprised Alesi on the opening lap. Hill would throw away his good work and the chance to wrap up the Championship at the start of the sixth lap, clipping a tyre barrier at a chicane, breaking the suspension and spinning out of the race. Fortunately for him, Villeneuve was to be significantly handicapped after also hitting the piled up rubber and finished seventh, so leaving the Englishman on the verge of the title.

This race came down to Alesi, long time darling of the 'tifosi', and Schumacher, the new Ferrarista. Michael closed and waited for the pit stops. The Benetton went in first and the extra two laps of fuel in the Ferrari's tanks proved decisive. Schumacher, with characteristic authority and judgement, produced sufficient pace to wrest the initiative. He re-emerged from the pits ahead of Alesi, as the explosion of approval from the grandstand confirmed.

A gap of four seconds stretched gradually and almost unerringly. A slight tremor went through the gallery when he brushed those unforgiving tyres, but he managed to hold on to the steering wheel and complete his mission 18 seconds ahead of Alesi. It was his third win of the season, his 22nd overall, and the first by a Ferrari driver here since 1988.

The faithful spilled onto the track in their thousands, their naked passion vindicated after all those years of hurt. They converged on the area beneath the podium, a mass of swaying humanity; like a field of poppies bobbing in the breeze. At the centre of this amazing scene was a giant, shimmering banner bearing the Prancing Horse. Schumacher leapt with glee and thumped the air. Victory for Ferrari at Monza is incomparable. Now he knew about emotion. He had been seduced by them just as they had been seduced by him.

Above Schumacher has a rear view of Alesi leading the frantic pack through first chicane at Monza, 1996, and *(right)* Michael escapes his brush with trouble

'It's crazy,' he said, 'just crazy. I've never seen emotion like it. It is only possible in Italy. I have goose bumps everywhere.'

Corinna, 14 weeks pregnant, and Michael's parents were there to share the thrill and pride. 'To win makes it the perfect day,' he said.

And perhaps even better days lay ahead. The following spring he was due to become a father and launch another challenge for the Championship. Others were stumbling over themselves to pick up his crown, but he remained imperious, his mantle as the greatest living racing driver probably more secure than ever.

Incomparable delight of winning for Ferrari at Monza.

Index

Photographic Acknowledgements

All photographs by Sutton Motorsport Images with the exception of those on pages listed below:
Michael Cooper/Allsport 142, 143:
Martyn Elford/Autosport 124, 124–5:
JohnTownsend/ Formula One Pictures 14R, 36, 53, 70, 76, 98–9, 102–3, 130–1:
Behram Kapadia 46, 47, 55, 60T, 91, 97, 107, 109, 112, 123T, 133T, 133B, 136:
LAT Photographic 2–3, 24, 30, 31, 32–3, 33B, 34–5, 54, 65, 90, 118T, 118B, 119, 120, 121, 142–3:
Mercedes-Benz 25:
Jad Sherif/Marlboro 9:
Sutton/Courtesy of Michael Schumacher Fan Club 15L, 15R, 16L, 16R, 19, 20T, 23T, 23B.